CONCILIUM

Religion in the Eighties

CONCILIUM

Concilium 189 (1/1987): Exegesis and Church History

CONCILIUM

List of Members

Advisory Committee: Exegesis

Directors:

Bas van Iersel SMM	Nijmegen	The Netherlands
Anton Weiler	Nijmegen	The Netherlands

Members:

Luis Alonso Schökel SJ	Rome	Italy
Josef Blank	Spiesen	West Germany
Settimio Cipriani	Naples	Italy
Aelred Cody OSB	St Meinrad, Ind.	USA
José Severino Croatto CM	Buenos Aires	Argentine
G. Del Olmo Lete	Barcelona	Spain
John Donahue ST	Berkeley, Ca.	USA
Jacques Dupont OSB	Ottignies	Belgium
José M. González-Ruiz	Malaga	Spain
Lucas Grollenberg OP	Nijmegen	The Netherlands
Paul Hoffmann	Bamberg	West Germany
Herbert Haag	Lucerne	Switzerland
Martin McNamara MSC	Blackrock, Co Dublin	Ireland
Roland Murphy OCarm	Durham, NC	USA
Jerome Murphy-O'Connor OP	Jerusalem	Israel
Franz Mussner	Regensburg	West Germany
Jerome Quinn	St Paul, Minn.	USA
Kazimierz Romaniuk	Warsaw	Poland
Rudolf Schnackenburg	Würzburg	West Germany
Heinz Schürmann	Erfurt	East Germany
John Scullion SJ	Parkville, Vic.	Australia
Elisabeth Schüssler Fiorenza	Cambridge, MA	USA
David Stanley SJ	Toronto, Ont.	Canada
Wolfgang Trilling	Leipzig	West Germany
Bruce Vawter CM	Chicago, Ill.	USA
Anton Vögtle	Freiburg	West Germany

CONCILIUM

List of Members

Advisory Committee: Church History

Directors:

Bas van Iersel SMM	Nijmegen	The Netherlands
Anton Weiler	Nijmegen	The Netherlands

Members:

Giuseppe Alberigo	Bologna	Italy
Joannis Anastasiou	Thessalonica	Greece
Roger Aubert	Louvain-la-Neuve	Belgium
Matthew Black	St Andrews	Great Britain
P. Bori	Bologna	Italy
Johannes Bornewasser	Tilburg	The Netherlands
Victor Conzemius	Lucerne	Switzerland
Enrique Dussel	Mexico City	Mexico
John Tracy Ellis	Washington, DC	USA
J. Kloczowski	Lublin	Poland
Jan van Laarhoven	Nijmegen	The Netherlands
Heinrich Lutz	Vienna	Austria
Giacomo Martina SJ	Rome	Italy
Heiko Oberman	Tübingen	West Germany
Bernard Plongeron	Paris	France
Emile Poulat	Paris	France
P. Siniscalco	Rome	Italy
Peter Stockmeier	Munich	West Germany
José Tellechea	San Sebastian	Spain
Brian Tierney	Ithaca, NY	USA

EXODUS—
A LASTING PARADIGM

Edited by
Bas van Iersel
and
Anton Weiler

English Language Editor
Marcus Lefébure

T. & T. CLARK LTD
Edinburgh

February 1987
T. & T. Clark Ltd, 59 George Street, Edinburgh EH2 2LQ
ISBN: 0 567 30069 2

ISSN: 0010-5236

Typeset by C. R. Barber & Partners (Highlands) Ltd, Fort William
Printed by Page Brothers (Norwich) Ltd

Concilium: Published February, April, June, August, October, December.
Subscriptions 1987: UK: £24.95 (including postage and packing); USA: US$45.00
(including air mail postage and packing); Canada: Canadian$55.00 (including air mail
postage and packing); other countries: £24.95 (including postage and packing).

CONTENTS

Part III
Contemporary Movements

Part IV
Evaluation and Hermeneutical Conclusion

CONCILIUM 189 Special Column

Hans Küng

The Hour of Truth for South Africa

THERE CAN be no denying it any longer: the time for radical changes in South Africa has come. Even the White Dutch Reformed Church has recently disowned apartheid, even though it has not yet begun to implement the inevitable practical consequences of this decision. It is true that Europeans and Americans are still far too unaware of a whole dimension of what is involved: the South African apartheid that was brought in as a result of the electoral victory of the National party in 1948 by a series of laws and bound up with enforced resettlements on a vast scale is the expression of a late outworking of the modern paradigm. For what is in question in South Africa is destitution effectively organised, deliberately administered and sophisticatedly brought about *by typically modern means, on the basis of a feeling of racial superiority, a Calvinistic awareness of election (on the part of 'the new chosen race': Buren), a capitalist profit-mentality and elements of German folk-thinking.*

The moment of truth has broken out, and not only for the Church leaders who stand behind the epoch-making Kairos Document of 1985. I have to acknowledge that I had not taken the situation in South Africa seriously enough myself. Before I saw the Black townships I was of the opinion that as a theologian one simply had to preach non-violence equally to Whites and Blacks. But this is not the reality. One cannot be even-handed as between oppressed and oppressors, exploited and exploiters; there can be no reconciliation between injustice and justice, good and bad; there can be no forgiveness without repentance, no repentance without removal of guilt and sin, repression and exploitation.

What many even White people passionately long for is a truly free, democratic, non-racial South Africa. *And despite the enormous tensions* many Blacks and Whites in South Africa are still convinced that violent revolution, even if successful, would lead to questionable results. The devilish circle of violence and counter-violence can be broken only if there is a readiness to negotiate on both sides:

— readiness on the part of the Whites to engage not merely in superficial 'reforms' but in radical changes of the social structures:

    i.   termination of the state of emergency;

    ii.   repeal of the race laws;

    iii. legalisation of the African National Congress (ANC);

    iv. freeing of political prisoners.

These are the pre-conditions for renunciation of violence on the part of the ANC and negotiation with the Black leaders. Finally, 'one man, one vote' will be as unavoidable as in any democratic State, and what this would mean in practice is a Black majority (there are 24 million Blacks or Coloureds over against 5 million Whites);

— readiness on the part of the Blacks, by way of response to the repeal of the race laws, the legalisation of the ANC and the freeing of political prisoners, to renounce violence and to start working for 'checks and balances' in view of a new democratic constitution and order, as in other democratic States, so as to forestall a new authoritarian and totalitarian State. There will have to be institutional guarantees not only for individuals but also for minorities (and not only the White minority but all the various racial groups).

    The most important things the Christian churches have to do are twofold:

— to work out and proclaim a spiritual-moral vision for the people: the vision of a new non-racist South Africa;

— to help in the elaboration of concrete political guidelines and alternatives (not blue-prints or finished plans) for the future of this country and this society, to be then translated into political reality by the politicians. What would be involved is a charter of basic rights, the model of a constitution, practicable proposals about the different sectors of public life (schools and so on). It is precisely Christians who, in the spirit of Jesus Christ, are capable of overcoming all resignation or cynicism, even when the struggle seems hopeless and the outcome at first very thin.

Translated by John London

EXODUS—A LASTING PARADIGM

Editorial:
Exodus—A Paradigm with Lasting Effects

THIS IS the first number to appear since the decision taken by the Committee for Exegesis and Church History to devote a joint number to both spheres of study. This formula certainly has the advantage of throwing light on the effects of Scripture on the subsequent history of faith. No one will surely take it amiss that the Editors and the Editorial Committee have chosen for this first joint number a subject that lends itself without difficulty to this new form of co-operation. Those who read this number will be able to confirm for themselves that the theological importance of the subject and its present relevance have remained intact as criteria. The fact that Exodus is a paradigm of lasting importance has everything to do with the fact that it expresses an experience that is closely related to one of the fundamental and lasting human needs, that of freedom and independence. The theme is particularly relevant now not so much because the situation with regard to freedom and independence is so much better or worse than it was, for example, a hundred years ago as because we are now much more sharply conscious of oppression, which is now much more general than it was in the past and is also felt not only in relatively new spheres, but also in relationships between men and women and in macro-economic and other new relationships.

This Editorial is followed by a brief review by *Roland Murphy* of the relationship between Scripture and the history of the Church. From the very beginning until quite recently, the author was one of the editorial directors of the section on exegesis and we are glad that he is willing to make it seen in this way that he is still one of us.

The theme itself is dealt with in four sections. The first is limited to the Scriptures, but even in this opening section something can be seen of the manner in which the event of Exodus becomes a paradigm. *Rita Burns*, for example, shows how the experiences of the people are expressed as a theme in the Pentateuch. *Erick Zenger* concludes that this theme is extended in the theme of the new Exodus in Isaiah, which was composed at the same time as the latest traditions of the Pentateuch. These reflections about the biblical data are rounded off with the article by *Jay Casey* on the elaboration of the theme in the Revelation of John.

Several of the later developments are reviewed in the second section. The post-biblical Jewish tradition is discussed—in a less specific way than the editors had in mind—by *Pinchas Lapide*. *John Newton* analyses a number of programmatic texts produced by differing movements in the Church, all of which appeal to the Exodus event. Weiler investigates the experience of similar communities. This section closes with an illuminating contribution by *Wesley Kort* about Leon Uris' novel *Exodus*.

The third section is devoted to contemporary developments in theology itself. *Enrique Dussel* discusses liberation theology, *Josiah Young* considers Black theology and *Dianne Bergant* looks at feminist theology. A structural model of the Exodus paradigm that is relevant for the other two forms of theology is developed in the theology of liberation.

The fourth section is more evaluative and hermeneutical in character. The sociologist *Baum* evaluates the effects of the Exodus paradigm on politics. The liberation theologian *Severino Croatto* throws light on the mutual effects of the Exodus theme on the history of liberation and of the experiences in that history on the interpretation of the relevant passages in the Bible. *David Tracy* finally attempts to make a theological evaluation.

As editors, we would not like to say whether this number is a successful example of what both exegetes and Church historians would like to achieve in co-operation. We would prefer to leave that judgment to our readers. One distinctive characteristic of this number, which emerged later but should have been easy to predict, is that it bears all the marks of a fugue. One after another, the different voices interpret the same theme at different pitch, with a different timbre and at a different volume. The result of this is, on the one hand, repetitions together with a striking unity and, on the other, fascinating variations and an underlying harmony. We do not, however, want to stress these aesthetic aspects too strongly. What is important is that the paradigm of Exodus is also valuable for the future because there will always be oppression and slavery and there will always be hope and liberation.

BAS VAN IERSEL
ANTON WEILER

INTRODUCTION

Roland Murphy

Scripture and Church History

THE UNDERLYING *raison d'être* for the union of Scripture and Church history was elaborated by Gerhard Ebeling in a study that dates back to 1947: *Church History as the History of the Exposition of Scripture.*[1] I have explored some of the implications of Ebeling's thesis elsewhere.[2] In this issue of *Concilium* it is particularly appropriate to give heed to his words:

> But interpretation of Holy Scripture does not find expression only in preaching and doctrine, and certainly not primarily in commentaries; but also in doing and suffering. Interpretation of Holy Scripture finds expression in ritual and prayer, in theological work and in personal decisions, in Church organisation and ecclesiastical politics, in the temporal power of the papacy, and in the ecclesiastical pretensions of rulers, in wars of religion, and in works of compassionate love ... (p. 28)

It is clear from the above that the 'exposition' of Scripture is to be taken in a broad sense. It deals with the 'Wirkungsgeschichte', or history of the effects that Scripture has produced on many levels throughout the history of the Church.

1. THE HISTORY OF THE EXPOSITION OF SCRIPTURE

Obviously no such 'history' can be presented here. Instead, we must call attention to certain factors which seriously affect the course of this history. The first is the *relatively late invention of printing* which made bibles available.

In one sense Ebeling's statement is best applicable to a literate society in which the Bible is a common possession. What is the 'history' before this modern situation? In the preceding ages Scripture was not a text that the average Christian explicated. This was the province of the educated, and hence usually the clergy. The Bible was appropriated by the believers through these teachers and preachers. Their expertise naturally varied a great deal. The giants among them, ranging from Origen through Augustine and Jerome, came to exercise enormous influence upon later generations. In the middle ages there appeared the style of the monastic *lectio divina*, and a somewhat rationalistic approach became evident as the Scripture was incorporated into the *Sentences*. This more or less academic transmission of the understanding of the Bible was filtered in various ways (preaching, liturgy, art, the *Biblia pauperum*) to the general body of the Church.

Second, it was assumed that the *Bible was identical with what one believed*. It was explained in the light of the tradition. As Augustine remarks in *De utilitate credendi* (14, 31): 'From whom did I derive my faith? I see that I owe my faith to opinion and report widely spread among the peoples and nations of the earth, and that these peoples everywhere observe the mysteries of the Catholic Church'. This assumption blunted the cutting edge of the Scripture as we would understand it today. Of course there were theological debates, as Gnosticism, Arianism, and other movements demonstrate. But the Bible played more of a confirmatory than exploratory role in all this. Theological thought, as it were, overpowered the analysis of the biblical text.

Third, the dominant hermeneutical position in Christianity was to *read the Old Testament in the light of the New*, especially from a typological point of view. This approach has not been rejected even today, as the famous *Old Testament Theology* (volume II) of Gerhard Rad reminds us. But the modern development in hermeneutics, in the understanding of the historicity and historical conditioning of an ancient text, has clearly checkmated an unbridled treatment of the Old Testament. The result is that over the last two centuries especially, Christianity has been able to hear the Old Testament more on its own level, and can now enter into a more profitable dialogue with the Hebrew Bible. Several examples could be given of this enriched understanding. One need only compare the *Moralia* on Job by Gregory the Great with the average current appropriation of this classic book in modern Christianity. For centuries the message of the Song of Songs was understood only on the level of God and people, Christ and the Church (or individual soul). Today it speaks on another level as well: to sexual human beings and their relationship in fidelity and love.

Fourth, one need not conceive of the influence of the Scriptures in *an individualistic sense*. It is not a question of an Augustine who confesses 'The message of your Holy Scriptures has set my heart throbbing, O Lord, and with the meagre powers that are mine in this life I struggle hard to understand it' (*Confessions* 12,1). The 'take and read' experience related in *Confessions* 8,12 is rather unique. There is no one text or one book that is primary. In the pages of this review (*Concilium* 7/2; September, 1966) Jean Leclercq has described the broad role of the Bible in the Gregorian Reform. In *Concilium* for September 1968 (7/4), G. Basetti-Sani described the Gospel vision of Francis of Assisi that affected both the life style of poverty and the attitude towards the Muslim. In *Concilium* for September 1969 (7/5), Y. Congar gave a hard look at the role played by the interpretation of the Old Testament in the clerical sacralisation of western society in the middle ages.

Finally, it seems obvious that much remains to be done in the relatively narrow field of the *history of biblical exegesis* itself. One can point to general summaries, and to specific studies, but these only scratch the surface.[3] Specifically, the *cultural presuppositions* of earlier interpreters need to be laid open. Here one learns both the reasons and the validity of the exegesis of earlier times. Twentieth century interpreters are not without their own presuppositions. It is shortsighted to write off earlier exegesis as precritical and benighted. One modern historian has remarked: 'The principal value of precritical exegesis is that it is not modern exegesis; it is alien, strange, sometimes even, from our perspective, comic and fantastical. Precisely because it is strange, it provides a constant stimulus to modern interpreters, offering exegetical suggestions they would never think of themselves, or find in any recent book, forcing them again and again to a rereading and re-evaluation of the text. Interpreters who immerse themselves, however, not only in the text but in these alien approaches to the text may find in time that they have learned to see, with eyes not their own, sights they could scarcely have imagined and to hear, with ears not their own, voices too soft for their own ears to detect.'[4]

But the analysis of earlier writers has to be in tandem with an historical exposition of movements within the Church, which were influenced in various ways by such interpretive processes. How were the Bible and biblical ideas communicated outside of the usual channels of liturgy and preaching? And what historical factors made certain biblical ideas more operative than others? These aspects did not escape Ebeling's attention:

The Church historian must pay a greater attention to the history of the interpretation of Holy Scripture in a stricter sense than has hitherto been the case: this may be either a more thoroughgoing use of Church history in the interpretation of individual passages, or by throwing light on the history of the understanding of individual sections or thought-patterns;

this may possibly take place not only in theological literature, but also in its practical interpretation of the event itself. (p. 29)

2. CHURCH HISTORY AS RADICAL CRITICISM

Ebeling closes his study with the remark:

The work of the Church historian operates as the radical critical destruction of all that, in the course of Church history, has interposed a barrier between us and Christ, instead of being an interpretation of Holy Scripture pointing to him. (p. 31)

He does not describe how the historian might go about this 'radical critical destruction'. But history has issued verdicts on many movements that have constituted a 'barrier' between the Church and Christ. One thinks here of the *temporal power of the papacy*—however apparently inescapable and imbedded in the historical development of the times it may have been. This and similar judgments are easier to make after the fact than in the maelstrom of events. But they do serve as a guide to the future 'pointing' to Christ.

The student of the Scriptures may affirm that the historian cannot work without the help of biblical scholarship. This provides a necessary criterion for sifting through the various movements that arise in the life of the Church. Biblical scholarship should not be conceived in a narrow sense, as if devoid of theological sensitivity. It is presumably part of the equipment of any Christian theologian, and is to be understood as referring to the results of the *historical-critical methodology* that is currently applied to the Bible. Despite the criticism often levelled against such an approach (the method is limited by its own presuppositions, etc.), it remains a solid criterion, and practically the only one, that enables the modern person to measure the validity of movements within the history of the Church. It is the surest means of unleashing the explosive power of the Word of God, so that the critical assessment envisioned by Ebeling can be achieved.

One has to come into the present century before a Roman Catholic theologian could state that the Bible is the '*norma normans, non normata* of both dogmatic and nondogmatic statements of faith'.[5] This statement of Rahner underlines the *cutting edge of Scripture* in the ecclesial assessment of traditions that have grown up in the Church. Let us consider some possible applications of it.

The critical question is this: *how faithfully has the Church heard the Bible?* This very issue of *Concilium* doubtless illumines various ways in which the

Church, or at least certain groups within it, have heard the Bible or failed to hear it. This is not the place to draw up pluses and minuses in the matter. But the Bible constitutes a kind of legal bar before which the events of Church history can be judged. While the Catholic tradition allows for the guidance of the Spirit in the history of the Church, this has obviously not eliminated grave mistakes (the persecution of Jews, the Crusades, etc.). In these cases the biblical word was twisted, or heard selectively, or simply not heard. Are there instances of this kind at the present time?

Biblical scholarship has been applied to *several critical issues* in recent times.[6] The bearing of the New Testament on the question of *divorce* has been studied carefully, but these views have not had much effect upon theology and practice.[7] The burning issue of the *ordination of women* emerges in the report of a task force of the American Catholic Biblical Association concerning the role of women in early Christianity: 'The conclusion we draw, then, is that the New Testament evidence, while not decisive by itself, points toward the admission of women to priestly ministry.'[8] This is not the only theological body to have registered such a view.[9] Admittedly a decision in a matter of this importance is not made overnight. But the 'tradition' of the Church should not be allowed to stand undifferentiated, even uninvestigated, as a decisive argument against biblical evidence.

The 'radical critical destruction' of which Ebeling spoke was partially realised in the reforms of Vatican Council II. At this writing (November 1985) there is a great deal of speculation about the meaning of the synod of Bishops convened in Rome to assess the Council. The brief period of the synod is in striking contrast to the length of the preparations and actual meetings of Vatican II. But taking stock of things is a necessary part of life, and in the case of the life of the Church, it is necessary to focus Scripture and Church history on the real issues. *Ecclesia semper reformanda ...*

Notes

1. *Kirchengeschichte als Geschichte der Auslegung der Heiligen Schrift* (Tübingen 1947); reproduced in *Wort Gottes und Tradition* (Göttingen 1964), and English translation in *The Word of God and Tradition* (Philadelphia 1964) pp. 11–31. Page references will be to the English translation.

2. 'Reflections on the History of the Exposition of Scripture' in *Studies in Catholic History in Honor of John Tracy Ellis*, ed. N. Minnich *et al.* (Wilmington 1985) pp. 489–499.

3. For historical sketches see *The Cambridge History of the Bible* ed. S. A. Greenslade *et al.* (Cambridge 1963–70) I–III; R. Grant and D. Tracy *A Short History of the Interpretation of the Bible* (Philadelphia 1984). The studies of Henri de Lubac

Exégèse Mediévale (Paris 1959–64) and Beryl Smalley *The Study of the Bible in the Middle Ages* (Notre Dame 1964) need to be supplemented.

4. David Steinmetz 'John Calvin on Isaiah 6' *Interpretation* 36 (1982) 156–170; 170.

5. K. Rahner 'What is a Dogmatic Statement?' in *Theological Investigations* (Baltimore 1966) V, 64; see also 'Scripture and Tradition' in *Sacramentum Mundi* ed. K. Rahner *et al.* (New York 1968–70) VI, pp. 53–57.

6. See Raymond E. Brown *Biblical Reflections on Crises Facing the Church* (New York 1975).

7. See the analysis, with complete bibliographical indications, of B. Vawter 'Divorce and the New Testament' *Catholic Biblical Quarterly* 39 (1977) 528–542.

8. The text is to be found in *Catholic Biblical Quarterly* 41 (1979) 608–613; the quotation is on p. 613.

9. Although no official word was issued, it seems that in the 1970s the members of the Pontifical Biblical Commission likewise found no scriptural warrant for the exclusion of women from priestly ministry.

PART I

Biblical Data

Rita Burns

The Book of Exodus

AT THE core of the Book of Exodus is theological testimony to God's solidarity with an oppressed people, a divine-human bond which replaces bonds of oppression with a covenantal bond and seals the solidarity of the liberating God with a liberated people moving into the future.

1. BACKGROUND CONSIDERATIONS

(a) Historical Background

The Book of Exodus is theological literature. To know about the historical events which constituted the raw material of the book's testimony, one must step beyond the theological screens surrounding these events. To do so is to engage in the task of historical recovery. It is to ask: 'What really happened?' Since none of the key events recounted in the Book of Exodus is firmly documented in extra-biblical sources, historians must resort to piecing together clues from biblical and non-biblical materials alike in an attempt to arrive at a plausible reconstruction of events. What follows is a brief survey of the results of such investigations.[1]

First, while extra-biblical materials never document *Israel's presence in Egypt*, they do show that it was not unusual for foreigners to go to Egypt, especially to the eastern border of the delta region, to make use of the resources created by the annual flooding of the Nile. Egyptian texts show that the empire offered terms for legal entry and access to fertile areas. Thus, the situation that brought the family of Jacob to Egypt, as described in the Book of Genesis, is a plausible one.

Second, scholars have found *evidence of Semitic influence in the Egyptian language*. Some research suggests that Semitic influence was especially prominent in the north-eastern delta region of Egypt, an area identified with the 'land of Goshen' where Israel's ancestors are said to have lived (Gen. 45:10; 46:28). At the same time, Moses and other figures from the exodus period (e.g., Hophni, Phinehas) bore Egyptian names. This two-way linguistic influence has been cited as evidence for the historical probability that Israel's Semitic ancestors really were in Egypt at the time of the exodus.

Third, Egyptian sources show that rulers of the Nineteenth Dynasty initiated *building activities* in the eastern delta region on the frontier of the empire. Construction began during the reign of Sethos II (c. 1305–1290) and was completed under Raamses II (c. 1290–1224). The project under construction was probably an estate of considerable size and included storage and administrative quarters as well as a royal residence. Egyptian sources call the residence the 'house of Rameses, beloved of Amun, great in victorious power'. Egyptian sources also indicate that those forced to work on this project included 'Hapiru (or 'Habiru or 'Apiru), people who lacked the civil rights enjoyed by citizens of the empire. Such groups were in Egypt between the fifteenth and twelfth centuries BC. This information from Egyptian sources parallels the biblical witness that Hebrew slaves were forced to build the store-cities of Pithom and Raamses (Exod. 1:11. Some linguists see similarities in the words 'Hebrew' and 'Habiru or 'Hapiru.). While extra-biblical materials do not specifically say that the ancestors of Israel were enslaved in Egypt, they do support the general authenticity of the situation described in Exod. 1:11.

Finally, if Exod. 1:11 is historically reliable it yields some direction in *dating the Exodus event*. The ancestors of Israel must have been in Egypt during the reign of Sethos and probably during the time of Raamses as well. The earliest extra-biblical reference to a people called 'Israel' appears on a stele from about 1220 BC which celebrates the victories in Palestine of Raamses II's successor, Merneptah. Many scholars link the evidence that (i) 'Israel' was in the land of Palestine near the end of the thirteenth century and (ii) Hebrews (read 'Habiru) worked on building projects under Raamses II. They conclude that the *Exodus took place in the thirteenth century BC*, probably in the early years of Raamses' reign.

The topic of greatest concern to the biblical writers is the *Exodus itself*. What can be said historically about the oppressed people's movement to freedom? Very little, if anything. The plague narratives probably had their origin in the cult tradition of passover. Although various locales for the sea crossing have been proposed, nothing can be said with certainty about the event at the sea as told in Exodus chs. 14–15. With the exception of Kadesh, the places in the Bible's wilderness itinerary are unknown. Egyptian materials pre-dating the Exodus link the word *yhw'* with nomadic groups in Arabia and some scholars posit that one such group brought the worship of Yahweh to Sinai prior to the Exodus group's trek through the wilderness. In fact, however, the biblical account of Israel's experience at Sinai-Horeb cannot be historically documented. The location of the mountain is unknown and there is no hard evidence outside the Bible to substantiate the biblical view that Israel's covenant and law originated there.

In conclusion, while it is impossible to document historically the testimony of the Book of Exodus, extra-biblical materials show that some of the situations described in the biblical text (especially the bondage in Egypt) are not at all unlikely. In the absence of historical proof, scholars are virtually unanimous in positing that there was *an actual event* in which some elements of the people later known as Israel left behind their status as subjects of an oppressive imperial government in Egypt and, with the leadership of Moses, came to freedom. This group (or its children), and perhaps others who subsequently joined it, brought into Canaan memories of the Exodus, of hardship in the wilderness, and of a profound encounter with the God, Yahweh, to whom the group bound itself in covenant.

(*b*) Literary Considerations

The final text of the Book of Exodus encompasses the perspectives of different generations each of which viewed the early stages of Israel's history as speaking to its own time. Adherents to the documentary theory of Pentateuchal composition detect at least *four literary sources* (J,E,D,P) in the book. Of these four accounts, the earliest (Jahwist, J.) and the latest (Priestly, P.) predominate.[2]

During the tenth century BC Israel enjoyed relative peace in a land of its own and assumed status among the nations as a kingdom under David and Solomon. During this period the Jahwist writers set out to tell how Israel had come to this 'golden age'. They traced Israel's success to the plan and fidelity of a promise-making God. For the Jahwist, the Exodus was a continuation of the story of promise begun in the Book of Genesis and completed when Israel reached the Transjordan as recorded in the Book of Numbers. The God of Exodus was Yahweh, 'the God of Abraham, of Isaac, and of Jacob' (3:16), who identified with Jacob's oppressed descendants in Egypt and came down to deliver them. Ultimately, Yahweh's purpose in the Exodus was to bring the Israelites to the land promised to their ancestors (3:7–8; 3:16–17). This God nurtured the Exodus group during its journey between the sea and Sinai (15:22b–25a) and then graciously forgave its infidelity after the covenant was made at Sinai (32:11–14). The mediator of Yahweh's grace was Moses (see especially 14:31 and 19:9) whose interaction with the Divinity was marked by frequent dialogue and who announced God's protest to pharaoh in prophetic fashion.

During the sixth century writers in priestly circles rewrote the Pentateuchal story for a generation which had lost its identity as a politically-independent people. The P writers addressed their community's need for a new self-understanding by reinterpreting the story of those generations who, like P's readers, were without land, nation or king. The priestly tradition viewed the Exodus as a new and definitive act of divine self-revelation (6:2–3) and as a means for both Israel and Egypt to know Yahweh (6:7; 7:5; 14:4,18; 29:46). In P's view, Yahweh brought the Israelites out of Egypt in order to dwell among them (29:46). P claimed that, in essence, Israel was a religious congregation made holy by Yahweh's 'tabernacling' presence (40:34–38) whose primary link with God was the cult. Thus P added to ancient legislation for the observance of passover (12:1–20) and drew on an old story about manna and quails in the wilderness to teach a lesson about sabbath (ch. 16). The covenant at Sinai was linked in a special way with the cult by the priestly writers' addition of concerns relating to the tabernacle and its cult (chs. 25–31, 35–40). Events connected with the Exodus were directed by a transcendent God's words which were faithfully executed by Moses and his priestly associate, Aaron, and ultimately by the entire community (39:32–43).

In conclusion, the Book of Exodus is a *complex fabric of literary traditions*, a tapestry bearing the convictions of storytellers, poets, cult officials, and lawyers from different generations each of which viewed the Exodus story as its own.

2. EXODUS FROM OPPRESSION

The opening chapters of the Book of Exodus describe a *spiraling movement of involvement in liberation*. The movement begins with women's acts of civil disobedience. It continues when the oppressed group cries out in protest over its situation. God hears the cry, identifies with the oppressed, and pledges to bring them to freedom through the mediator, Moses, who voices the divine protest to pharaoh. Following a long struggle, pharaoh releases the oppressed.

(a) Initial Stages (1:1–7:7)

The oppression of Israel in Egypt is presented as a matter of life and death. An unnamed pharaoh views the burgeoning life of his Hebrew subjects as a threat. Fear prompts the ruler to try to bring his subjects under control by laying heavy burdens on them. Ironically, life among the oppressed continues to increase (1:8–12).

The king's thoughts turn to death. He commands the midwives, Shiphrah and Puah, to kill the Hebrews' sons but to let their daughters live. (Note that in this and the incident which follows, it is females who subvert the tyrant's plans!) Liberation begins with two women's refusal to participate in oppression. The midwives fear God, not pharaoh. What began as a story about death is thus transformed into a story about birth. Even the midwives have families! (1:15–21).

Civil disobedience continues during the third and final stage of oppression (1:22–2:10). Death is now full-fledged State policy. All pharaoh's people are commanded to cast Hebrew boys into the Nile (but again, 'you shall let every daughter live'). The biblical text features the response of one Hebrew woman and two daughters, her own and pharaoh's. The writer borrows the outline of a legend which once described the remarkable beginnings of Sargon, an ancient Mesopotamian ruler. According to the legend, the baby who would grow up to be leader was placed in a protective basket in a river from which he was rescued. In the Hebrew retelling, the baby is Moses who will eventually 'draw out' Israel from Egypt (see 2:10). Into the outlines of the ancient story, the Hebrew writer has inserted a sister who brings together Moses' mother and pharaoh's daughter, both of whom act with courage and compassion. Pharaoh's daughter adopts Moses, even though she is aware that the baby is a Hebrew and on her father's death-list. Once again, life prevails as women join one another in refusing to participate in State-sponsored oppression.

A new stage in liberation begins with the Hebrews' consciousness of their oppression. Their cry of protest triggers a profoundly new era, a stage signalled by a literary construction which draws readers' attention to the subject of the verbs: 'God heard ... God remembered ... God saw ... God knew ...' (2:23–25). The Divinity joins the group protesting its oppression.

Once involved, God chose Moses to be the spokesperson of the divine protest and the divine resolve to deliver the oppressed. The cooperative divine-human mission was forged at Horeb-Sinai. Moses, having made his own exodus from Egypt, is called back to the solidarity with the oppressed which he had demonstrated prior to his mysterious encounter with God (see 2:11–22). The biblical writer uses the form of a prophetic call narrative[3] to show that the Exodus was not simply the result of a great social activist's zeal. Moses returns to Egypt as a messenger representing God's commitment to Israel's liberation.

The revelation of the divine name is cast within the context of Moses' call (3:13–15; and see 6:2–3). The biblical writers voice their theological conviction that Israel learned God's name in the Exodus event. That is to say, in moving toward liberation, Israel came as close as it would ever come to knowing the true identity of God. Whatever the proper translation of the enigmatic statement commonly rendered 'I am who am', Yahweh is the God who delivers from oppression: 'This is my name for ever, and thus I am to be remembered throughout all generations' (3:15).

(b) Plagues, Passover and Passage (7:8–15:21)

Even with divine involvement, the movement from bondage to freedom does not take place quickly or easily. It comes to a halt when Moses issues God's protest to pharaoh: 'Let my people go.' God summons pharaoh to join in the movement which would free the oppressed but the oppressor retains a firm grip on his subjects even in the face of an unequivocal divine imperative. Thus, a difficult struggle ensues. Among the wonders communicated in the plague narratives is the depth of an oppressor's resistance to the divine imperative of 'letting go'.

The account of the tenth plague is divided into two parts: the plan is announced in 11:1–10 but its execution is delayed until 12:29–39. The two parts form a literary enclosure around legislation for the observance of passover, the feast of unleavened bread, and the consecration of the firstborn. In later generations these rituals provided a cultic point of entry for Israelites who sought to make the liberation experience of Exodus their own.[4]

While the narrative of the tenth plague has elements in common with the preceding plague stories, it also bears features which suggest that this plague is a radically different action on God's part. In place of the command, 'Let my people go', is a simple announcement of the death of Egypt's firstborn (11:1–10). At the end of the lengthy section of legislation, the account of the night of passage (12:29–39), like the event it narrates, is brief and decisive. The pharaoh's death-dealing (chs. 1–2) descends upon him and his empire and the tyrant expels the Israelites (12:31–33).[5]

Literary tension abounds in the narrative account of the event at the sea (ch. 14), an indication that different generations sought to convey their own perspectives. One strand highlights the human perspective (pharaoh's plans, Israel's fear) while another features the divine (divine word spoken and fulfilled). One strand presents a miraculous occurrence (waters like walls) whereas another describes an act of nature (a strong east wind). A battle motif runs throughout, the two sides of the conflict being the Egyptian armed forces and Yahweh who alone does battle with the Egyptians (14:14). However it is told, the biblical account of the event at the sea conveys the Israelites' conviction that Yahweh delivered them from the Egyptians. In the text, the event at the sea is cast as the final and definitive act of the deliverance from Egypt.

This event, like the night of passage, was celebrated ritually by later generations. Readers catch a glimpse of early celebrations in 15:20–21 where Miriam leads the women in a dance and hymn celebrating Israel's divine warrior. Appropriately, liberated women lead the celebration of the freedom which began when women refused to participate in oppression and which was fully realised through Yahweh's solidarity with the oppressed.

3. LIFE IN THE WILDERNESS

Exod. 15:22–18:27 treats the Exodus group's journey from the sea to Mount Sinai.[6] In these wilderness narratives, separate traditions have been brought together through literary use of itineraries. The aetiological character of these stories is clear. The incidents at Marah, Massah and Meribah explain how those places got their names (15:22–25a; 17:1–7). Ch. 17:8–16 legitimates Israel's ongoing feud with the Amalekites. Ch. 18 explains the origin of a system for the administration of justice in a later period.

The desert is a wild territory where survival requires that travelers have a sense of direction. It is an appropriate setting for biblical writers to present basic theological convictions about Israel's source of life as a free people and about what maintaining that life of freedom would require of them: *trust, simplicity, and justice*.

Where does life come from if not from pharaoh (16:3; 17:3)? In the desert, security in bondage seems preferable to the precariousness of freedom and Israel directs its hostile regrets at Moses who interprets them as complaints against Yahweh (16:8; 17:2). The need for water and food becomes a test of divine reliability: 'Is the Lord among us or not?' (17:7). The Divinity graciously provides for Israel's needs through Moses' intercession. Yahweh not only delivers from oppression but also sustains life in freedom.

Ch. 16 presents a detailed scheme of how Yahweh nurtures, i.e., day by day. The writers also use the custom of sabbath rest to teach about the requirements of a life sustained by gift as opposed to a life dependent on slave wages. Yahweh's gift of food serves as an opportunity for Israel to learn a responsible lifestyle. Daily provisions satisfied each person's need; no more, no less. Some failed in the discipline of living one day at a time (v. 20). Others could not let themselves rest when the time came (v. 27). Both excesses were counterproductive. Grasping and greed go against the nature of freedom. They are contrary to life founded in gift and trust, the characteristics of Israel's life with Yahweh.

The manna story begins with remembering the good old days at pharaoh's table (16:2–3) and ends with a cultic directive designed to replace memories of slave wages with memories of God's gifts (16:32–33). When future generations think of sustenance, they must recall the 'daily bread' of the wilderness, not the 'fleshpots' of Egypt. They are to trust the *precariousness of freedom, not the security of bondage.*

Finally, ch. 18 unfolds in two scenes, both of which feature Jethro, Moses' Midianite father-in-law.[7] In the first (vv. 1–12) the biblical writers focus on Jethro's enthusiastic endorsement of Yahweh as the One who delivered Israel from oppression. In the second (vv. 13–27) Jethro initiates systemic changes in the way justice is administered in the Israelite community. At the point of Jethro's intervention, Moses' role in community leadership seems to be both singular and complex. He decides sacred matters as well as civil disputes (vv. 15–16). Jethro suggests that this is a poor use of resources and a burden for all involved (vv. 14, 18). To expedite matters, he advises decentralisation of leadership which, he says, is God's command (v. 23). The two themes in the chapter are connected: *Yahweh as liberating God and the community's ready access to justice.* The freed community must organise itself in such a way as to ensure that all continue to have access to the justice initiated by Yahweh in the Exodus event.

4. THE SINAI EVENT

The biblical writers say that, along the way between the coming out of Egypt and the coming into the land, the Exodus group journeyed to the mountain where Yahweh had first spoken to Moses. Like Moses, the Israelites met Yahweh at Sinai in an encounter which shaped their interactions with God and with others for all time. In their account of this event, the biblical writers include the covenant between God and Israel (chs. 19–24), a story of infidelity and forgiveness (chs. 32–34), and the construction of the tabernacle as the mode of God's continuing presence with Israel (chs. 25–31, 35–40).

(a) Covenant and Law

According to biblical tradition, Sinai was the place where Israel was invited to *formalise its relationship with Yahweh.* The relationship had already been forged in the Exodus event. Sinai provided the opportunity to establish that relationship as a formal bond extending into the future. God initiated the encounter (see the theophany of ch. 19) and instructed Israel in its responsibilities in the ongoing relationship (see the laws of chs. 20–23).

According to ch. 24, Israel swore on oath to accept its responsibilities and the relational bond was ritually sealed through symbols rich with suggestions of shared life (see the meal and the sprinkling of blood in 24:1–11).

In the biblical account, the focus of the Sinai covenant is the law. The biblical writers collected generations of Israel's civil, moral and cultic laws, attributed their origin to God, and placed them within the context of Yahweh's liberating work. The One who upset pharaoh's order thus establishes a new one. The law expressed how the Israelites would respond in an ongoing way to the One who delivered them from bondage. *Freedom would have direction*. The conjunction between Exodus and Sinai witnesses to the theological connection between *freedom and fidelity*.

The law begins with the self-identification of the law-giver: 'I am the Lord your God, who brought you out of the land of Egypt, out of the house of bondage.' Israel's law, then, is *theocentric* in character. It flows out of the person of the God who liberates. The community belonging to this God must express in concrete situations its bond with its covenant partner, Yahweh.

As apodictic law, the decalogue is categorical in nature and addresses matters of ultimate concern, matters on which the life of the community was thought to depend. It seeks to protect *core values* in the life of the community, charting boundaries which rule out those things which endanger the common life. At the head of the list is the command that Israel be characterised by undivided loyalty to Yahweh. The wholeness of the community rests in the Oneness at its centre. There follow laws which spell out how Israel's loyalty would take shape in the interactions of community members. Community wholeness required the mutual respect of persons, justice.

Many of the laws contained in the so-called Covenant Code (20:22–23:33) were probably borrowed from the customs of Israel's ancient Near Eastern neighbours. There are some, however, which are more firmly rooted in Yahwistic faith (see 20:22–26 and 22:18–23:19).[8] The latter group requires exclusive worship of Yahweh and a social structure consistent with God's liberation of the oppressed. Israel is directed to recall its life in bondage and thus to pay special attention to the justice due to powerless groups within the community: widows, orphans, strangers and the poor.

(b) Covenant Broken and Restored

The biblical writers suggest that the covenant story was incomplete until it addressed *Israel's infidelity and God's forgiveness*. Enveloped by concerns relating to the tabernacle (chs. 25–31 and 35–40), chs. 32–34 reflect the view that Israel's ongoing covenantal bond with Yahweh was maintained not so much by human fidelity as by divine mercy.

Moses' prolonged absence sparked the community's demand for certainty that God was with them. Aaron willingly fashioned the calf which was worshipped as the God who brought Israel out of Egypt. This failure in trust struck at the heart of the freedom sustained by Yahweh. The initial divine reaction was to blot out the whole community and start over again with Moses (32:7–10), but through Moses' intercession that reaction was modified (32:11–14, 30–35). Once Moses was sure of God's pledge to continue with Israel, he inquired further about the character of God's ongoing presence. Readers are reminded of Moses' first encounter with Yahweh at Sinai-Horeb where Moses sought access to the divine character through knowledge of the divine name (ch. 3). Now Moses pleads: 'I pray thee, show me they glory' (33:18). In the wake of the calf incident, Moses asks God: 'Let me see again who you are, now that you know who we are, an unfaithful people.' Although Israel had changed, the theophany narrated in ch. 34 shows that the name is constant. the God who restores covenantal relationship with Israel is still Yahweh but at this point Israel learns new implications of that name. Yahweh is 'a God merciful and gracious, slow to anger, and abounding in steadfast love and faithfulness' (34:6) and also the One who requires justice: '... who will by no means clear the guilty' (34:7). The name thus holds in dynamic tension the mysterious balance of *divine mercy and justice.*

(c) Yahweh's Tabernacling Presence

Chs. 35–40 describe how God's instructions for the tabernacle (chs. 25–31) were carried out through the community's cooperative efforts. However, the writers testify that Israel's tabernacle was not simply the work of human hands. The closing verses of the Book of Exodus narrate Yahweh's coming to the tabernacle (40:34–38). Thus, the intention for the tabernacle announced in 25:8 was fulfilled: 'And let them make me a sanctuary, that I may dwell in their midst.' According to the priestly writers, the tabernacle was to be the centre providing orientation for Israel's life in the future.[9]

The closing chapters of the Book of Exodus attest to Israel's conviction that the God of Exodus, wilderness and Sinai would continue in solidarity with Israel. Ch. 29:45–46 says that this was the goal of the entire Exodus story:

And I will dwell among the people Israel, and will be their God. And they shall know that I am the Lord their God, who brought them forth out of the land of Egypt that I might dwell among them; I am the Lord their God.

Notes

1. See J. Bright *A History of Israel* 3rd ed. (Philadelphia 1981) pp. 120–129; S. Herrmann *A History of Israel in Old Testament Times* (Philadelphia 1975) pp. 56–85 (*Geschichte Israels in alttestamentlicher Zeit* München 1973); M. Noth *The History of Israel* 2nd ed. (New York 1960) pp. 110–121 (*Geschichte Israels* 1950); see T. L. Thompson 'The Joseph and Moses Narratives: Historical Reconstructions of the Narratives' *Israelite and Judean History* ed. J. H. Hayes and J. M. Miller (Philadelphia 1977) pp. 149–166.

2. The Elohist account probably originated in the northern kingdom during the ninth century BC. Only fragments of this version appear in the final text. The Deuteronomic circle made a few additions to a combined form of the J and E works during the seventh or sixth century BC.

3. Call narratives typically contain these elements: (a) divine confrontation; (b) introductory word by the Divinity; (c) divine commission; (d) objection by the person called; (e) reassurance by the Divinity; and (f) sign given by the Divinity. See the structure of 3:1–12.

4. Ritual practices of bloodsmearing, eating unleavened bread, and offering firstborn shaped the biblical writers' account of the night of Israel's passage out of Egypt.

5. See 14:5a: 'When the king of Egypt was told that the people had fled …'.

6. Numbers chs. 10–22 treats the movement from Mount Sinai to the plains of Moab in the Transjordan. While the two groups of wilderness traditions share common motifs, stories in Numbers typically present Israel as a stiff-necked people dissatisfied with the way things are. Yahweh responds with anger and punishments. This differs from the need-gift pattern of Exod. chs. 15–18.

7. Like 17:8–16, ch. 18 stands apart from the rest of the wilderness narratives in Exodus in so far as there is no itinerary notice, no need expressed by the people, and no record of God's life-sustaining gifts along the way. However, the concern about community offices addressed in 18:13–27 in some way anticipates leadership controversies belonging to the wilderness narratives of Numbers chs. 10–22.

8. See P. Hanson 'The Theological Significance of Contradiction within the Book of the Covenant' *Canon and Authority* ed. G. W. Coats and B. O. Long (Philadelphia 1977) pp. 110–131.

9. These Exodus texts, written in a late period, reflect the P writers' familiarity with the Jerusalem temple where the tabernacle came to rest (1 Kings 8). The writers project back into an early period their vision of the cult as the primary locus for the experience of God.

Erich Zenger

The God of Exodus in the Message of the Prophets as seen in Isaiah

1. THE EXODUS OUT OF THE DESERT OF GOD'S DARKNESS

WITH THE sack of Jerusalem in 586 BC and its political consequences the people of JHWH were plunged into a *catastrophe not only of historical, but primarily of theological and political moment*. The Exodus 'credo', that narrative calling-to-mind of past deliverance which had enabled Israel to master the innumerable crises and calamities of its pre-exilic history, now was itself profoundly shattered. That JHWH saves his people from military embarrassment, looks with favour on the oppressed and exploited small farmers, liberates his people from the enslaving forms of worship of other gods, and that he led Israel out of Egypt to make of it a clan that he would protect in a special way—all this had now become highly questionable. Was Exodus only an episode after all? And was it a mere illusion to interpret it as a revelation of the abiding favour of JHWH to Israel? Is the power of JHWH himself in fact limited? Has he turned away from Israel? Is his relationship with Israel at an end, and will he even create a different people for himself?

Isaiah 40–55, 60–62, which came into being in several stages partly in Babylon and partly in Jerusalem, endeavours to deal with these questions which plagued both those deported to Babylon and those remaining in the mother country (e.g. Isa. 40:27; 49:14). Here the *Exodus tradition becomes a central theme* in a vision of salvation which exercised a strong influence on the formation of the Book of Isaiah right up to the third century BC[1]—a process which joined Isa. 40–55, 60–62 to Isa. 1–39. While the Exodus tradition played

22

no part in the thought of the historical prophet Isaiah, it becomes a constant and unifying theme in the final form of the Book of Isaiah.[2]

The attempt to regain the Exodus 'credo' begins in Isa. 40–55, 60–62, where the 'worm Jacob' (Isa. 41:14), 'deeply despised, abhorred by the nations, the servant of rulers' (Isa. 49:7) is the recipient of a revelation of the glory of JHWH 'in the desert' (see Isa. 40:3–5)—the decisive act of salvation. Whereas in Ezekiel 'the wilderness of the peoples', into which JHWH had brought his people after the catastrophe of 586, is the place of judgment upon the people of JHWH (see Ezek. 20:35f.), in Isa. 40–55 the desert is the place where JHWH's lifegiving nearness will show itself in a special way (see also Jer. 31:21). In a conflation of traditions which is typical of this prophecy, 'the wilderness' now actually becomes the precondition for JHWH's demonstration of his unique, special power and faithfulness—as once in the first Exodus from Egypt. On the one hand, the desert is the traditional topos for ultimate danger and the annihilation of life, but, on the other hand, the Sinai tradition which sees the desert as the place of the divine revelation is so enriched with themes from creation theology that the experience of catastrophe now becomes the condition for the new and authentic revelation of JHWH.

The programmatic opening of this vision proclaims the (new) advent of JHWH to his people in the desert:

In the wilderness prepare the way of the Lord,
make straight in the desert a highway for our God.
Every valley shall be lifted up, and every mountain and hill made low;
the uneven ground shall become level, and the rough places a plain.
And the glory of the Lord shall be revealed,
and all flesh shall see it together,
for the mouth of the Lord has spoken. (Isa. 40:3–5)

This passage makes no mention of the exit or destination of this highway, nor does it say that the road is to be built for the people. On the contrary, a way is to be prepared *in* the desert (not *through* it!) on which JHWH can appear. Nor is it said whence JHWH will come. What is decisive is not where JHWH comes from but the purpose of his coming: he is to reveal himself in the hopelessness of desert, exile and catastrophe. On the one hand the theme of 'preparing the way' stresses the aspect of JHWH's 'coming'. JHWH comes to his people which is 'in the desert'. On the other hand it also underlines the inner quality of this coming. Here the prophetic vision takes its imagery from the preparation of roads for the planned journey of a king so that he can travel with the ease appropriate to his rank. Thus all obstacles are to be removed, the road is to lead through level country—and the king's arrival is to be visible from far and wide. All mortals must be able to see his glorious appearance; that is why the location of his epiphany is to be transformed into a vast, wide and even plain.

In the linking of Exodus theology and creation theology in Isa. 41:17–20 it is made clear that the purpose of the manifestation of God's glory in the desert is to *bring Israel's distress and suffering to an end* by enabling it to recognise and accept JHWH once again as the Saviour-God who bestows his special favour upon it. First of all Israel's situation in the exile is spoken of in the same terms as its situation in Egypt. The Israelites are 'afflicted, wretched and poor'. This is how Exod. 3:7 and Deut. 26:6f. refer to the socio-political exploitation by the Pharaonic state; JHWH delivered the people by causing the flight of the slaves to succeed and the representatives of the regime of death to drown in the waters of the Red Sea (Exod. 14; Deut. 26:8). Isa. 41:17 describes the 'poverty' of Israel in exile metaphorically: '... when the poor and needy seek water, and there is none, and their tongue is parched with thirst'. The metaphor takes up the theme of Exod. 17:2 but expands that particular situation into a general situation of calamity characterising the desert. JHWH brings this desert situation to an end by coming to the desert himself (Isa. 40:3–5): when he turns to the afflicted, a fullness of paradisal life is opened up to the Israel that was threatened with extinction (Isa. 41:18f.). Contrary to a frequently heard view there is no mention here of JHWH miraculously providing the returning exiles with water and shade, so that wherever they go springs will gush forth and trees suddenly sprout. Such an interpretation takes the metaphor as reality—a reality which failed to materialise, as most commentators are obliged to add. This is a misunderstanding of the prophet speaking in Isa. 41:17–20. He is not some deluded fortune-teller but a prophet recounting his vision of JHWH's coming to the 'poor' in images drawn from his tradition and incorporating new graphic elements. Calling on this tradition, he reminds his contemporaries who are suffering the eclipse of God during the exile (Isa. 42:18–20) of the experienced reality of the God of Israel. By implying, through the use of metaphor, that this reality is thoroughly relevant to their 'desert' situation, he is endeavouring to create the forward thrust of a vision of hope. The prophet has a threefold aim with his metaphor of God's desert advent: (*a*) to help them to see the catastrophe not as the end of JHWH's history with his people but as a crucial stage of this history; it is a wilderness in which JHWH can prove himself to be the God of Exodus by showing favour to the poor. (*b*) Since the metaphor is rooted in historical experience it cannot be dissolved in the world of mere ideas or dreams. (*c*) By using this metaphor he is able to give his vision that openness and plasticity which will leave room and freedom for God to create something 'new' here in the desert (see Isa. 42:9; 43:19; 48:6) which, while it is in continuity with what went before, also represents the renewal and re-establishment of what had lost its power and vitality.

2. THE NEW GOD OF THE NEW EXODUS

JHWH gives something new to his people, but this does not mean that it is to replace or take over from something old, nor does it imply that what is happening has never happened before.[3] God's new deed which the prophet sees and proclaims is not the beginning of something new and previously non-existent, but *a new and renewing beginning.* Here 'new' means 'young and sprouting' like vegetation after the winter rain (see Isa. 42:9; 43:19). The 'new' coming of JHWH to his people 'in the wilderness' is not a qualitatively different coming compared with his coming in the earliest history of Israel. But it is new in that it puts an end to the desert stage of catastrophe in which God hides his face:

Thus says the Lord, who makes a way in the sea,
a path in the mighty waters,
who brings forth chariot and horse, army and warrior;
they lie down, they cannot rise,
they are extinguished, quenched like a wick:
'Remember not the former things,
nor consider the things of old.
Behold, I am doing a new thing;
now it springs forth, do you not perceive it?
I will make a way in the wilderness and rivers in the desert.
The wild beasts will honour me, the jackals and the ostriches;
for I give water in the wilderness, rivers in the desert,
to give drink to my chosen people,
the people whom I formed for myself' (43:16–21).

The tripartite composition, which adopts the pattern of an oracle of salvation, shows the situation which is to be transformed by this word from the God of Exodus. The crippling fixation of Israel, 'the blind and deaf servant of the Lord' (see Isa. 42:18–20) on the catastrophe and its consequences, the tendency to look back, which no longer brings liberation, the fatalistic apathy that puts up with the *status quo* and turns to the great saving deeds of the past only for ideological distraction from the painful present—the prophet confronts these pointless attitudes and fears with the vision that JHWH is *still the God who is always doing a new thing.* The seed he sowed at the beginning of Israel's history will continue to yield a harvest. The 'former things', i.e., the judgment situation of the exile,[4] is at an end for Israel since a new tree is growing from the trunk that was cut off. Israel must realise this. Israel must allow its eyes to be opened for something apparently impossible, namely, that there is a way leading out of the desert and that in this desolation streams of water are already running at which Israel can satisfy its thirst and draw strength. This vision however, aimed at turning Israel's gaze to the future, has its roots in the past. Salvation is announced explicitly by the God of Exodus who prepared a path of safety through the midst of the waters of the Sea of Reeds—whose chaotic and deadly aspect is underlined by the formula 'in the great, mighty water-floods'—and extinguished the gigantic military machine of Pharaoh's pursuing army 'like a wick'. The text uses participial apposition to refer to the first Exodus, i.e., 'making a way ...', 'bringing forth chariot and horse ...'; Exodus is not quoted as an event concluded in the past: rather *JHWH's action at the Exodus is seen as profoundly characteristic and continuously constitutive of his nature* (the participle is durative); it is the foundation on which Israel's history rests and which brings a 'new thing' into being. Since JHWH has in some degree defined himself, through the events of the Exodus, as the Saviour who makes a path for Israel, he will rejuvenate his history with Israel for the sake of his own identity. Just as in the first Exodus he was not hindered by Pharaoh's army, so now there is no political or mythical power that can frustrate or prevent the work he intends to do. The 'new thing' the God of the Exodus is now undertaking is not simply a repetition of what happened at the beginning. The first Exodus involved the annihilation of Israel's enemies, but this destructive aspect has now faded away. The prophet addresses the people of God that has been 'wasted' by wars and deportations, proclaiming a 'new' Exodus God who will end Israel's suffering without the use of war and destruction. This peaceful miracle of the new Exodus which will lead Israel out of the desert is so spectacular that the 'denizens of the wilderness' will hold JHWH in awe because of it. Jackals and ostriches, whose dirge-like howling and moaning in the desert seems to symbolise a world hostile to man (see Mic. 1:8), now sing the praises of JHWH because he has turned to his people to renew them. Whereas the first Exodus was marked by the corpses of the Egyptians who were extinguished like a wick, the new Exodus is actually applauded even by 'jackals and ostriches'. This new Exodus transforms the world of nations. Its central, theological figure is drawn in ideal terms in the four Songs of the Suffering Servant of God (Isa. 42:1–4, 5–9; 49:1–6, 7–9; 50:4–9, 10–11, 52:13–53:12), whose activity is explicitly contrasted with that of the God of the first Exodus by the fact that he 'will not quench a dimly burning wick' (Isa. 42:3). Another metaphor puts it like this: JHWH changes the darkness of Israel's desert into light (Isa. 42:16) so that Israel can become 'a light to the nations' (Isa. 42:6; 49:6).

The skilfully constructed disputation between Israel and JHWH in Isa. 51:9–16 establishes that JHWH's new Exodus plan does not aim at the destruction of Israel's enemies but at Israel's renewal, i.e., regaining its identity as the people of JHWH.⁵ It begins with the nation challenging JHWH to repeat the first Exodus, but in even greater proportions:

Awake, awake, put on strength,
O arm of the Lord;
awake, as in days of old,
the generations of long ago.
Was it not thou that didst cut Rahab in pieces,
that didst pierce the dragon (Tannin)?
Was it not thou that didst dry up the sea (Yam),
the waters of the great deep (Tehom);
that didst make the depths of the sea a way
for the redeemed to pass over? (51:9–10)

Here, in the terminology of war, Israel appeals to JHWH, the mighty victor in the primal struggle of the gods, to liberate his redeemed people in a new battle. Just as he slew the chaotic powers of the water, Rahab and Tannin, at the beginning of creation and appointed limits to the other two primal hostile powers, 'sea' (Yam) and 'great deep' (Tehom), so that the creation should have a firm and protected dwelling place,⁶ now he should once more annihilate Israel's enemies (which are his enemies too) in accordance with his being and power. The first Exodus is referred to here as the triumph of JHWH in combating primal chaos, stressing even more that the new Exodus is seen as a *replay of the original struggle between the gods*. As Ps. 87:4 and Isa. 30:7 show, Rahab is also a mythical metaphor for Egypt; according to Ezek. 29:3, 32:2, Tannin similarly stands for Pharaoh. Thus in this summons to the 'arm of JHWH', itself a metaphor for JHWH the Warrior, the Israel of the exile calls for a new Exodus as a revelation of JHWH after the pattern of the battle in which JHWH annihilated the primal enemies of creation (Rahab and Tannin) and the prime enemy of Israel, Pharaoh. Replying to his people, JHWH takes up this appeal to unlimited power but gives it a new direction intended to wean Israel away from all ideas of a strong God who destroys the others; he wants Israel to discover that he is a loving God who wants to bestow new life, firstly and foremostly to Israel:

I, I am he that comforts you;
who are you that you are afraid of man who dies ...
and have forgotten the Lord, your Maker ...
and fear continually all the day because of the fury of the oppressor ... ?
He who is bowed down shall speedily be released;
he shall not die and go down to the Pit,

neither shall his bread fail.
For I am the Lord your God ...
stretching out the heavens and laying the foundations of the earth,
and saying to Zion, 'You are my people.' (51:12–16)

In his reply JHWH appears most definitely as the transcendent Lord of heaven
and earth. But he does so without having recourse to the mythology of the
struggle of the gods. Indeed, he actually reveals the baneful effect this theology
of war has had on Israel itself. Israel's fear of its enemies led it to forget JHWH
its God. Those for whom victory or defeat are the only alternatives are easily
led by historical realities to declare JHWH a loser. Here God opposes the
picture of JHWH the Warrior and of a new Exodus that would annihilate
enemies, with the reality of *JHWH the Consoler who reminds Zion of the
Covenant promise*, still valid but now renewed: I am your God and you are my
people. That is the innermost core of the new Exodus: JHWH turns to Zion
like a loving mother in a personal relationship, in order to bring Zion out of its
forgetfulness of God and fear of the surrounding world (Isa. 49:14). Israel's
liberation begins with the renewal of the Covenant promise to Israel in exile.[7]
God answers the fearful Israelites who stridently call for the epiphany of the
God of war, but he intends to reveal himself in the reality of the Covenant
lived out by his people on Zion. The servant Israel cries for vengeance, but in
reply JHWH puts forward the picture of the *Suffering Servant* who, by
renouncing power and accepting suffering, becomes a witness to the power of
reconciliation and love that can change the world (see esp. Isa. 50:4–9;
52:13–53:12).[8]

So that Zion may become the place of the theophany of the God of Exodus,
JHWH himself will accompany the exiles back into Jerusalem. Thus *Zion
becomes the 'new' Sinai* on which JHWH appears, commences his reign and
promulgates his royal law. This vision can be discerned in Isa. 40–55 and in the
'continuation' (Isa. 60–62), but it was also taken up in an early post-exilic
edition of Isa. 1–39 and deliberately inserted to set the stage at the beginning of
the Book of Isaiah in Isa. 2:1–5.

In the herald's instruction which JHWH gives the bringer of good tidings to
Jerusalem/Zion in Isa. 40:9–11—which must be understood as a development
of the process of consolation initiated in 40:1 (see Isa. 51:12)—while JHWH's
saving advent is still portrayed with a reference to the Exodus from Egypt
(40:10: 'Behold, the Lord God comes with might, and his arm rules for him';
see e.g. Deut. 4:34; 5:15; 7:19; 11:2; 26:8; Exod. 20:33f.), yet, as in Isa. 51, the
image of the God of war or the victorious general is transmuted into that of the
caring shepherd of his people. Similarly, in Isa. 52:7–10, which directs our gaze
away from the herald and the watchmen and towards the ruins of Jerusalem

which are to break forth in shouts of joy, the advent of JHWH to Zion is portrayed as a realisation of his kingly reign, its manifesto summed up in the word *shalom* (52:7). In JHWH's 'speaking peace to his people' (52:9) the world-transforming condition of *shalom* has begun to take effect on Zion, that peace which JHWH intends to manifest 'to all the ends of the earth' and 'before the eyes of all the nations' (52:10), radiating from Zion. Once again the theme of the 'arm' is taken over from the tradition of the struggle of the gods and the Exodus battle and transformed in a 'pacifist' sense: the new Exodus which is to promote the peace of the nations takes place under the sign of JHWH's *'holy* arm', which he wields in a special way for the sake of his people.[9] A later addition, drawing out the consequences of this message of consolation to Zion/Jerusalem for those Israelites living in the Diaspora, once more emphasises the constrast with the first Exodus from Egypt:

Depart, depart, go out thence,
touch no unclean thing;
go out from the midst of her, purify yourselves,
you who bear the vessels of the Lord.
For you shall not go out in haste,
and you shall not go in flight,
for the Lord will go before you,
and the God of Israel will be your rear guard. (52:11f.)

Here, in deliberate antithesis to the tradition of the first Exodus (see Exod. 12:30; Deut. 16:3), the new Exodus does not have to take the form either of escape from a prison camp or slave compound or of the flight of the remnants of a defeated army. The new Exodus is a peaceful, solemn procession, once more described with a metaphor from pastoral life: 'whereas the shepherd at the head has to show the way, the shepherd who brings up the rear keeps the animals together'.[10] JHWH performs both functions simultaneously; significantly, JHWH the Shepherd once again replaces JHWH the Warrior described in the first Exodus.

3. ZION RENEWED: AN ESCHATOLOGICAL SINAI FOR THE NATIONS OF THE WORLD

A scattered Israel returns to a Zion that has been renewed by conversion and righteousness (55:6f.), where JHWH himself bestows the fullness of life (55:1–3). This return constitutes an 'everlasting sign' not least because it takes place 'in joy and in peace' (55:12). Even the nations participate in this Exodus by bringing the sons and daughters of Mother Zion home in their arms and on their shoulders (49:22). The nations are caught up in the dynamism of the new Exodus and actually make their own way to Zion to experience the reign of JHWH there and learn his royal law from an *eschatologically renewed Israel* (55:4f.). That is why JHWH chose Israel as his son in the first Exodus; this is the task which was being prepared for Israel through the catastrophe of exile and through Israel's political powerlessness in post-exilic times, namely, to give an example to the nations of the justice and righteousness of JHWH (Isa. 42:1, 4). The new creation of Israel 'in the wilderness' of its suffering is to make Israel a veritable incarnation of the Torah for the nations:

> Listen to me, my people,
> and give ear to me, my nation;
> for a law will go forth from me,
> and my justice for a light to the peoples. (Isa. 51:4)

An initial portrayal of the vision of the *procession of nations* to Zion is to be found in Isa. 60:1–62:7. This passage is 'a creative continuation of Isa. 40–55 ... beginning with the theme of the return home in 55:12f. Isa. 60:1 continues the summonses to Zion already found in 51:17ff., 52:1f. and 54:1ff., and Isa. 60 and 61 continue Isa. 40–55. (Isa. 60 is an address to Zion; in 61 Zion speaks concerning the population and towns of Judah after the pattern of Isa. 40:1ff.; 9ff.) These two chapters are supplemented by the speech of JHWH in Isa. 62:1–7 which deals with the problem of evident delay'.[11] At the beginning of this composition the P-document vision of JHWH's glory which appears over Sinai—thought of as the mountain of the creation of the world (see esp. Exod. 24:16f.)—is transferred to Jerusalem (Isa. 60:1–3). The kings and nations of the earth flock to this place of eschatological divine presence (60:4–10). Not only do they bring rich gifts with them, they voluntarily offer their services to make Jerusalem a perfect 'city of God'. The nations which formerly afflicted Israel with sword and spear now work as 'ploughmen and vinedressers' for the people of God (60:10, 14; 61:4–5).[12] What is this glory that shines over Jerusalem, the eschatological Sinai, and which the nations seek to share? Isa. 61:1–3 puts it in a nutshell: those who dwell there are (evergreen) 'oaks of righteousness'. Upon Zion lives a free, happy society, the glory of JHWH. The 'new Jerusalem' is a place where JHWH causes a lived righteousness to spring forth (61:11), so that the nations observe it and say: Thus is God! For the present, of course, this is 'only' a prophetic vision, but its fulfilment is dear to the heart of JHWH:

> For Zion's sake I will not keep silent,
> and for Jerusalem's sake I will not rest,

until her vindication goes forth as brightness,
and her salvation as a burning torch.
The nations shall see your vindication,
and all the kings your glory. (62:1f.)

The idea that a *renewed Zion is to become the Sinai of the nations* where they will learn the Torah of JHWH is put forward in Isa. 2:1–5.[13] Thus Israel is given a definite mediating role. The Torah 'which goes forth from Sinai/Zion' is aimed at enabling the nations to live together without violence and war and for their mutual benefit:

And they shall beat their swords into ploughshares,
and their spears into pruning hooks;
nation shall not lift up sword against nation,
neither shall they learn war any more. (2:4)

This re-thinking of the role of the nations leads to a worldwide policy of peace; it is the reaction to the fact that Zion has become 'the highest of the mountains' because the people of God who dwell on it 'walk in the light of JHWH', i.e., live out JHWH's peace-bringing Torah of brotherhood and righteousness, renouncing violence and practising supportive love (Isa. 2:5). This is the service Israel will now perform for JHWH on his holy mountain. Different from the first Exodus is the fact that *at the centre there no longer stands the cult but the social and political ethos*. Israel will thus become a 'witness to the peoples' (Isa. 43:10; 55:4; 19:20) by its exemplary life, the goal of the eschatological exodus from the desert of its forgetfulness of God. Israel is to be a 'missionary' to the nations, not by going to them but by living as the servant of JHWH in brotherly love and peace. In a final redaction, in the third century, there is a further return to the Exodus tradition to set forth the vision of an *eschatological festal table-fellowship* of Israel and all the nations; in it, the God of the Exodus will reveal and demonstrate himself to be the good King of Sinai/Zion. Now, in allusion to the Sinai tradition of the glory of JHWH upon the mountain, where the elders had a vision of God and shared a meal on Sinai (See Exod. 19:24),[14] we read:

Then the moon will be confounded (because of its pale light),
and the sun ashamed,
for the Lord of hosts will reign on Mount Zion and in Jerusalem
and before his elders he will manifest his glory.
On this mountain the Lord of hosts will make for all peoples
a feast of fat things,

a feast of wine on the lees ...
And he will destroy on this mountain the covering that is cast over all peoples, the veil that is spread over all nations. He will swallow up death for ever, and the Lord God will wipe away tears from all faces, and the reproach of his people he will take away from all the earth; for the Lord has spoken.' (Isa. 24:23; 25:6–8)

With the eschatological dawn of God's reign on Sinai/Zion the times of mourning and suffering on the part of the nations are over; as for Israel, its period of being despised and persecuted by the nations has ended. Indeed, as a further elaboration puts it: even death itself will be deprived of its power. According to this prophetic theology the judgment of JHWH, which is now applied to all the nations of the world as a precondition of universal salvation, does not aim at destruction, but at knowledge of JHWH and conversion. In its affliction Israel will call to JHWH, who will send a new Moses to complete the eschatological work of salvation (see Isa. 19:20b and Exod. 3:7–10). No longer do the eschatological plagues upon 'Egypt' and 'Assyria', the two enemies par excellence of the people of God, bring about desolation and death as in the first Exodus (see Exod. 7–14): now 'the Lord will smite Egypt, smiting and healing, and they will return to the Lord, and he will heed their supplications and heal them'᾿(Isa. 19:22). Then 'Egypt' and 'Assyria' will join with Israel, God's possession, and become one 'people of God' as a result of Israel's lived witness: 'In that day Israel will be the third with Egypt and Assyria, a blessing in the midst of the earth' (Isa. 19:24; see similarly Zech. 8:13).[15] The revelation of JHWH as the God of the Exodus, which began with Abraham (see Gen. 12:1–3) and was continued in the first Exodus is aimed at creating *a Covenant fellowship of peace among all nations, mediated by Israel's exemplary way of life*. Israel's first liberation from the Egyptian house of bondage looks towards the abolition of all the 'houses of bondage' known to history; this will come about when all nations realise and accept that they are fellow table-guests of the good King JHWH.

Translated by Graham Harrison

Notes

1. On the general hypothesis indicated here regarding the evolution of the Book of Isaiah see O. H. Steck *Bereitete Heimkehr. Jesaja 35 als redaktionelle Brücke zwischen dem Ersten und dem Zweiten Jesaja*. Stuttgarter Bibelstudien 121 (Stuttgart 1985).

2. See also W. Zimmerli 'Der "neue Exodus" in der Verkündigung der beiden grossen Exilspropheten' in his *Gottes Offenbarung. Gesammelte Aufsätze zum AT*

(Munich 1963) 192–204; K. Kiesow *Exodustexte im Jesajabuch. Orbis Bibl. et Orient.* *35* (Fribourg-Göttingen 1979); H. Simian-Yofre 'Exodo en Deuteroisaias' in *Bib 61* (1981) 530–533.

3. For this understanding of 'new' see esp. Ch. Levin 'Die Verheissung des neuen Bundes' in *Forsch. Rel.u. Lit AT und NT 137* (Göttingen 1985) 138–141.

4. For other interpretations, see K. Elliger, *Deuterojesaja* I *Bibl. Komm.* XI/1 (Neukirchen 1978) pp. 350–354.

5. This interpretation follows Th. Seidl 'Jahwe der Krieger—Jahwe der Tröster. Kritik und Neuinterpretation der Schöpfungsvorstellungen in Jesaja 51:9–16' in *Bibl.Not. 21* (1983) 116–134.

6. See E. Zenger 'Gottes Bogen in den Wolken' in *Stuttgarter Bibelstudien 112* (Stuttgart 1983) 81–84.

7. See the theology of the 'new Covenant' also present in Jer. 31:31–34; Ez. 36:24–28.

8. See esp. E. Haag 'Die Botschaft vom Gottesknecht—ein Weg zur Überwindung der Gewalt' in *Gewalt und Gewaltlosigkeit im Alten Testament* ed. N. Lohfink (Freiburg 1983) 159–213.

9. Contrary to the more usual, 'militaristic' interpretation of the text, e.g. B. Duhm *Das Buch Jesaja* (Göttingen 1968) p. 392.

10. B. Duhm p. 393.

11. O. H. Steck (see note 1 above) 69.

12. In the evolution of the text this idea may have been the stimulus for Isa. 2:4.

13. See the summary of literature in R. Kilian *Jesaja 1–39. Erträge d. Forsch. 200* (Darmstadt 1983) 86–91.

14. See P. Welten 'Die Vernichtung des Todes und die Königsherrschaft Gottes. Eine traditionsgeschichtliche Studie zu Jes. 25:6–8; 24:21–23 und Ex. 24:9–11' in *Theol. Zeitschr. 38* (1982) 129–146.

15. This idea is also linked with the reign of God from Zion in Ps. 47:10.

Jay Casey

The Exodus Theme in the Book of Revelation Against the Background of the New Testament

'AND THE Lord brought us out of Egypt with a mighty hand, and an outstretched arm, with great terror, with signs and wonders; and he brought us into this place and gave us this land, a land flowing with milk and honey' (Deut. 26:8–9). This confession of the Jews' faith and understanding of the Exodus is shared by John, the author of Revelation. With the Jews, John agreed that the Exodus involved God's redemption of Israel, his judgment upon her oppressors, and his granting of an inheritance to the nation.

But John departs from the Jewish understanding of the Exodus when he proclaims that it is not history, even sacred history but a hope fulfilled in Christ, and a paradigm of God's continuing activity on behalf of his people. So in the midst of Revelation's apocalyptic images of cosmic evil and struggle there can be detected John's conviction concerning the continuing meaning of the Exodus: God remains his people's redeemer, the judge of their oppressors, the guarantor of their eternal inheritance.

1. THE EXODUS THEME IN THE PRESENTATION OF REDEMPTION

In two passages John's presentation of the Christian's redemption reflects the influence of the Exodus. The first is Revelation 1:5–6. Like much of Revelation, this is the language of worship, very likely originating in the context of baptism. One can detect the influence of Psalm 88 (LXX) behind the honorific titles attributed to Christ in verse five. Also evident is the Christian

34

exegesis that re-identified the Messiah whom Judaism called 'the firstborn' as, 'the firstborn *from the dead*'.

This small Christology of Jesus as the one crucified, resurrected, and ascended is supplemented by three statements of praise (vv. 5b–6a) in which Jesus' death is presented as a redemption on the order of, but greater than, the Jews' redemption from Egypt. By his reference to Christ as, 'the one who loosed us from our sins by his blood', John draws the reader's attention to the Old Testament's conceptions of the efficacy and power of the sacrificial blood. But by the addition of the phrase from Exodus 19:6, 'and made us a kingdom, priests to his God and father', John, without denying the significance of Jesus' death effecting atonement, cleansing, or sanctification, given priority to the understanding of that sacrifice as the blood shed for the liberation of humankind from sin to serve God as kings and priests, a holy people. Jesus' sacrifice is that of a new and greater paschal lamb, whose redemptive death effects a new and greater exodus.

This presentation of redemption is developed further in a second passage, Revelation 5:9–10. In the larger context of the enthronement of the Messiah as ruler of the Kingdom of God, John's image of the Davidic, messianic king (5:5–6) has been qualified by the identification of the lamb as one slain (v. 6). This one's worthiness to execute God's judgment by opening the sealed scroll depends on his sacrifice that, at the cost of his blood, effected the purchase of people from all the earth. This image from the marketplace, suggesting the manumission of slaves, is used in the New Testament in connection with the redemption of Christians (I Cor. 6:20; 7:23; I Pet. 1:18; 2 Pet. 2:1).

The citation of Exodus 19:6 in the following verse reveals again that John's image of the Lamb is controlled by the paschal lamb tradition, rather than the lamb as presented in Isaiah 53, or the lamb of the daily temple sacrifice. This citation of Exodus 19:6 differs from that in Revelation 1:5–6, with the words 'kingdom' and 'priests' now being connected by 'and' and thus relating appositionally.

But it is the addition in verse ten of the phrase, 'and they shall reign upon the earth', that adds a new and important element to this image of redemption. The phrase serves to emphasise the motif of authority rather than the people's sacerdotal identity. As elements of the Christian's inheritance, these will be discussed more fully below. It is well to note, however, that the reign of the saints here and in Revelation 20:4–6 and 22:5 forges a strong link between Revelation's presentation of redemption and inheritance. Nevertheless, while the redemption pictured in 1:5–6 is related to individual sin and the acquisition of the dignity and authority of kings and priests, the emphasis in 5:10 is on a broader redemption of humankind that leads to their reign in the messianic kingdom. In both instances, the redemption from among humankind of a people to become a kingdom and priests to God is effected by the sacrifice of the Lamb and is presented in a pattern moulded by the Exodus tradition of redemption.

2. THE EXODUS THEME IN THE PRESENTATION OF JUDGMENT

Through the three series of visions symbolised in the seals, trumpets, and bowls, John presents a picture of God's judgment on those who oppress his people. The Exodus traditions make a significant contribution to this presentation, especially in the trumpet (8:6–11:19) and bowl (15:5–16:21) series of judgments.

Form critical studies of the entire bowl series and of the first four trumpet judgments indicate that they are modeled on the Egyptian plague narratives (H. P. Müller, 'Die Plagen der Apokalypse. Eine formgeschichtliche Untersuchung *Zeit fur die neu. Wissenschaft* 51 (1960) 268–70). In addition the treatment of the Exodus plague tradition in the Wisdom of Solomon appears to have exercised significant influence on John, especially in his emphasis on the intention of the trumpet judgments being to bring about rebellious humankind's repentance rather than destruction (9:20–21).

To these structural and conceptual similarities can be added several shared elements between the Exodus plague tradition and the trumpet judgments of Revelation.

The sounding of the first trumpet (8:7) results in the raining of hail and fire mixed with blood upon the earth. As a consequence, a third of the earth, trees, and green grass are consumed. Similar consequences attended the seventh Egyptian plague (Exod. 9:23ff.), in which men, beasts, plants and trees were struck down by hail accompanied by thunder and fire from the sky.

The second trumpet's judgment (8:8–9) is presented as the casting into the sea of a great burning mountain that turns a third of the sea into blood, killing a third of the creatures of the sea, and destroying a third of the ships. These consequences may reflect the first Egyptian plague, when Moses turned the Nile into blood (Exod. 7:20ff.).

The third trumpet judgment (8:10–11) resembles the second, except that in naming the fallen star 'Wormwood', John recalls Jeremiah 9:15 and 23:15 where water made bitter by wormwood is a symbol of divine punishment. But this reverses the pattern of Exodus 15:23, where Moses made the bitter waters of Marah drinkable for the people of God.

The fourth trumpet produces a judgment of limited darkness. Similarly, in the ninth Egyptian plague (Exodus 10:21ff.) 'thick' darkness covered Egypt, but lasted for only three days. Though it appears in only the first four of the series, the Exodus tradition is an obvious component, along with mythical and apocalyptic themes, in John's presentation of judgment through the trumpets.

It is noted above that the use of the Exodus plague tradition in the Wisdom of Solomon supplied John with material and conceptions for his fresh employment of these traditions in the presentation of judgment. In the bowl judgments, the Wisdom-based notion that the divine wrath is intended to induce repentance (see Exod. 9:16–17; Revel. 9:20–21) and not destruction is abandoned, and another Wisdom-based conception is substituted. Specifically, the bowl judgments reveal John's collation of one's punishment with one's sins, an idea propounded in Wisdom 11:15–16. For example, in the first bowl judgment (16:2) those marked with the sign of the beast are afflicted with bodily sores. In the third (16:4f.) those who have shed the blood of the saints are forced to drink from rivers and springs which have been turned into blood. The doubling of the first Egyptian plague (the defiling of the Nile) provides the basis for the second and third bowl judgments. This doubling in Revelation 16:3–7 results in the universalisation of the effects of the plague so that all the waters of the earth are fouled.

Exodus associations, beyond the formal structure already noted, are not so apparent in the fourth and fifth of the bowl judgments, but do reappear with the sixth bowl. There the angel's bowl dries the Euphrates (16:12) to open a way for the 'kings of the East'. It was expected that in the messianic age the Euphrates would be dried for Israel's return to the Promised land (Isa. 11:15: Zech. 10:11; II Esd. 13:47). But in this judgment scene, the significance of redemption through the parted Red Sea is reversed as the dried Euphrates becomes a way leading to evil's final destruction.

In the conclusion of the sixth bowl judgment, with the froglike spirits (16:14), and then in the seventh bowl scene with the 'plague of great hailstones' (16:21), the influence of the Exodus plague tradition can again be detected. Evident in these two instances is John's tendency throughout his presentation of judgment, whether in the trumpet or bowl series, to apply the Egyptian plagues eschatologically and to embellish them with apocalyptic features which give them a universal range and ultimate significance.

3. THE EXODUS THEME IN THE PRESENTATION OF INHERITANCE

The promise of inheritance is the most complex of the three elements of the Exodus theme which John has appropriated and developed in Revelation. In three passages which share a common setting in heaven (7:1–17; 14:1–5; 15:1–5) John employs the Exodus traditions to portray the meaning of the Christian's inheritance. Then in three additional passages (20:1–6; 21:1–8;

21:22–22:5) the content of that inheritance is portrayed more specifically and completely.

(a) The Meaning of the Christian's Inheritance

(i) *Revelation 7:1–17*

While this passage begins with a vision of the people of God on earth (vv. 4–8), it concludes with the multitude in heaven (vv. 9–17). In the initial vision two features are of particular interest for the consideration of how the Exodus traditions have influenced John. One of those is the 'sealing' of God's servants upon their forehead (v. 3). The use of seals in the ancient world was widespread, especially as marks of possession, identification, and signs of authority. Slaves and soldiers were tatooed on the arm or forehead with their owner or ruler's mark. In Ezekiel 9:4ff. those who are marked on their forehead are saved from physical death in the outpouring of God's wrath on Jerusalem. In Revelation 7:3 however, the mark serves not so much as a guard against physical death but as a pledge of security during the end-time calamities and against the coming demonic threats (see 20:4–6). John's use of the Egyptian plague tradition in the presentation of judgment against the oppressors of God's people would suggest that the inspiration for the sealing of God's servants here may come from the Exodus story of the protection of Israel from the effects of the Egyptian plagues (Exod. 8:22f.; 9:4; 10:23). Particularly noteworthy was their deliverance from the angel by the sprinking of their doorposts with the blood of the Passover lamb (Exod. 12:ff.).

The second salient feature of this passage encourages this association of sealing with an Exodus-based redemption, i.e., the use of the tribes of Israel as an analogy for the Church (vv. 5–8). In Revelation 7:14ff. this same throng is described as having been redeemed by the Lamb and enjoying an inheritance based on the promises of the Exodus. In Revelation 14:1–5 the Church is again symbolised by the 144,000. They appear there with the name of the Lamb and the Father on their forehead, as the redeemed from the earth.

In the second vision of Revelation 7 the 144,000 become in heaven a vast throng from 'every nation and all tribes, peoples, and tongues' (v. 9). The distinguishing feature of this multitude is their white attire, robes the possession of which throughout Revelation is the result of having been redeemed by the Lamb (7:14; 3:5; 19:8, 3–14), and having been granted an inheritance as his (6:11; 22:14). The specific content of that inheritance can be seen in verses fifteen through seventeen. The multitude's presence before the throne of God reverses the Exodus tradition prohibition concerning the impossibility of seeing God face to face (Exod. 19). Their inheritance also means that they gain a priestly vocation in fulfilment of the Exodus promise

(Exod. 19:6) mediated to them through their redemption by the Lamb (Rev. 1:5–6; 5:9–10; 21:7; 22:3). This vocation is described as follows: 'and they serve him day and night in his temple' (v. 15a). The basic intent of the Exodus (see Exod. 6:6–7; Lev. 26:11–12; Deut. 14:2) is fulfilled as the people stand in the presence of God, offering priestly service to him, and dwelling in his glory and presence.

(ii) *Revelation 14:1–5*

In this passage the 144,000 previously identified as the Church redeemed by the Lamb and serving him in heaven (7:1–17) now stands with the Lamb, the leader of God's people, on Mt Zion. This passage merges the notions of a priestly vocation and kingly rule. These images John found in Exodus 19:6 and used in Revelation to describe Christian redemption (1:5–6; 5:9–10). Here they add another glimpse of the meaning of Christian inheritance. That additional aspect of inheritance includes the knowledge given to the redeemed to sing the 'new song' (14:3), a knowledge appropriate for ones granted intimate and unobstructed fellowship with God.

The description of the 144,000 in verses four and five as ones who 'have been redeemed from mankind as first fruits for God and the Lamb', suggests yet another connection with the Exodus tradition. The tribe of Levi is designated in that tradition (Num. 3:11–13; 8:14–18) as the 'first fruits' of Israel that Yahweh has consecrated as his own. Like the 144,000 of Revelation 14:5, these priests were required to be without blemish (Lev. 21:17, 18, 21, 23). Again in fulfilment of Exodus 19:5–6, the 144,000 on Mt Zion stand as a new, redeemed, consecrated priesthood. This priestly vocation is the strongest link in Revelation between the themes of redemption and inheritance, both of which originate in the Exodus tradition.

(iii) *Revelation 15:1–5*

This heavenly scene of the conquerors at praise beside the sea is obviously inspired by the traditions of Israel's song of praise at the Red Sea (Exod. 15; see Deut. 32). The order of the vision even follows closely the Exodus text. In other passages the multitude of the redeemed has been identified as ones sealed (7:4), or ones bearing God's name on their foreheads (14:1). Here their identification as the 'conquerors' (v. 2) and as ones singing the 'song of Moses, the servant of God, and the song of the Lamb' (v. 3), ties together these three visions and makes synonyms of 'sealed', 'bearing God's name', and 'conqueror'. This linking of the song of Moses and the song of the Lamb also demonstrates unmistakably John's appreciation of the Exodus as a paradigm of the redemption now come in Christ.

(b) The Content of this Inheritance

(i) *Revelation 20:1–6*

In this passage as well the double-faced destiny of the believer is again described as a fulfilment of the Exodus promise: 'they will be priests of God and of Christ, and they will rule with him a thousand years' (v. 6). That this promised inheritance has been found elsewhere in Revelation to be the possession of all the redeemed (7:14–15) would suggest that the martyrs of this passage are not given special reward during the millenium, but rather enjoy first the privileges (see 22:4) given all those whom the Lamb has redeemed (1:5–6; 5:9–10).

(ii) *Revelation 21:1–8*

The venerated tradition of Jerusalem—Zion as the eschatological city of salvation is a controlling influence in this presentation of the new creation. But embedded in the climactic vision of the new heaven and new earth are two images which suggest that the character of the new creation is an embodiment of promises first made in Exodus. The first is in verse three, where the heavenly city is described as 'the dwelling of God with men'. Going beyond the city's identification, the phrase denotes its ultimate meaning. God's 'tabernacling' with the people represents the reality of unhindered and unbroken fellowship, a quality of fellowship first promised in the Exodus tradition (Exod. 3:12; Lev. 26:11–12). The appearance of the new Jerusalem also brings into reality the personal relationship of God and his people ('and they shall be his people', v. 3). This too represents the fulfilment of a fundamental promise of the Exodus story (Exod. 6:7; Deut. 14:2; 26:18–19), and along with the image of God's dwelling with the people, presents the redeemed as God's possession who enjoy his presence eternally (22:3–5).

The second Exodus-based image appears in verse seven. There John summarises all the promises so far offered with the provision that 'the one who conquers will inherit these things (i.e., dwelling with God, the absence of tears, sorrow, and pain, sustenance from God's living water, vv. 3–4, 6), and I will be his God and he will be my son'. This gathering of inheritance's many features into the consummate meaning of a filial relationship with God has been attributed to the influence of the Davidic traditions of the Old Testament (2 Sam. 7:14), especially as developed in the messianic-royal tradition (Ps. 89:26–27). While this realisation calls to mind the promises to the conqueror in Revelation 2 and 3, the notion is set in a passage which describes clearly the realisation of the whole people's destiny as God's people (v. 3). This fulfilment of the individual's redemption in sonship thus becomes a feature of that corporate inheritance. In coalescing the Davidic and Exodus traditions in the presentation of the inheritance of the people, John repeats the combining of the same two traditions in the presentation of redemption in Revelation 5, where redemption is accomplished by 'the root of David, ... the lamb who was slain' (5:5–6).

(iii) *Revelation 21:22–22:5*

In this passage John moves the reader into the inner recesses of the new Jerusalem. The portrayal is a product of many sources, with the Exodus tradition being particularly evident. The first indication of this influence comes in the opening verses of the first vision when the new Jerusalem is said to hold no temple because God and the Lamb are its temple (21:22). This is the conclusion to John's insistence that the end of inheritance is God's dwelling with the people himself (21:3) and their continual presence before him (7:15). This completion of what was lacking in the Exodus is effected by the Lamb's presence in the eschatological city of Zion, establishing it as the city of his redeemed (21:27).

In the second vision (22:1–5), John describes the realities of life in the new Jerusalem as fulfilling Ezekiel's prophecy of the new Temple (Ezek. 47:1–12) and regaining the life lost in Eden (Gen. 3:22–24). The river of life has its source, however, in the throne of God and the Lamb (v. 1, 3). It is around that life-giving throne that 'his servants shall worship him: they shall see his face, and his name shall be upon their foreheads ... and they shall reign for ever and ever' (vv. 3–5). Already in Revelation 7:1–17 a proleptic vision has been offered suggesting that an identity (marked with God's name) and vocation (priestly worship) is the inheritance of those redeemed by the Lamb. This vision now confirms that previous one; the eschatological inheritance of the redeemed is their privilege to serve as priests before God himself, and to reign eternally. This is what the Exodus promised but what the redemption of the Lamb accomplished—'You shall be to me a kingdom of priests and a holy nation' (1:5–6; 5:9–10).

To this picture John adds, 'they will see his face' (v. 4). This vision of God's face is the fulfilment of all the aspirations of the Old Testament cult, and the elimination of its most distinctive restriction (see, Exod. 33; Lev. 16). To say that the redeemed priests-kings-servants of God 'will see his face' means that they each enjoy forever what no one had previously been allowed—continuous, face-to-face fellowship with God. The power of the image rests in its gathering up all the promises of the Exodus: that the people would be a kingdom of priests; that God would dwell with them; that they would be his people and he would be their God.

In summary, then, one can identify several Exodus-based themes which describe John's understanding of the meaning of inheritance: knowledge and fellowship with God (14:1–5; 22:3–4); identity and vocation (7:4; 14:1; 21:3;

22:4; 1:5–6; 5:9–10; 20:6); sustenance and comfort (7:3; 9:4; 16:2); life (7:9; 20:15; 21:27; 22:1–2).

4. THE CHARACTER OF REVELATION'S USE OF THE EXODUS THEME

The use of the Exodus theme in Revelation is an example of typological interpretation. Biblical typology is a prophetic mindset which is expressed in literary form when the tradition-characteristic conceptions, episodes, descriptions and language of God's previous redemptive actions are employed to describe his continuing redemptive activity. Typology is characterised by: historical continuity between the type and its antitype; an intensification in the antitype of the salvific action associated between the two; a christocentric unity; a creativity often associated with poetry or art (see P. Joseph Cahill 'Hermeneutical Implications of Typology' *CBQ* 44 (1982) 273ff.).

The use of the Exodus theme in Revelation is clearly of this kind and should be designated as typology. The character of John's use of the Exodus in a typology of redemption, judgment, and inheritance also distinguishes his employment of the Exodus theme from that found elsewhere in the New Testament. In Mark one finds an order to the Gospel traditions which reflects a typological appropriation of the Exodus theme. In the book of Hebrews, Exodus typology can be seen influencing the writer's Christology and ecclesiology. The conviction, throughout the New Testament, that the Church is the new Israel is an example of Exodus typology. Numerous other single-element examples of the use of Exodus typology in the New Testament could be cited (e.g., 1 Cor. 5:7; 10:1–11; Rom. 3:24; 2 Pet. 2:5, 9–10; John 6).

These uses are to be distinguished from John's use of this typology in Revelation. There the Exodus tradition does not only serve as an organising pattern for his visions, nor simply as a source for illustrative details in presenting his prophecy. For John the Exodus is the event which orders and gives shape to his hope. To understand the meaning of redemption, the consequence of oppressing God's people, and the content of Christian inheritance, John turns to the intentions and activity of God first revealed in the Exodus. These, he says, are, 'what must soon take place' (Rev. 22:6).

Select bibliography

Court, J. M. *Myth and History in the Book of Revelation* (John Knox Press 1979).
Fiorenza, E. S. *Priester Für Gott. Studien zum Herrschafts—und Priestermotiv in der Apokalypse* (Aschendorff 1972).

Goppelt, L. *Typos: Die typologische Deutung des Alten Testaments im Neuen* (C. Bertelsmann 1939).

Holtz, T. *Die Christologie der Apokalypse* (Akademie Verlag 1962).

Journals:

Fiorenza, E. S. 'Redemption as Liberation: Apoc. 1:5f. and 5:9f.' *CBQ* 36 (1974) 220–32.

Osten-Sacken, P. v. d. ' "Christologie, Taufe, Homolagie"—Ein Beitrag zu Apc. Joh. 1:5f.' *ZNW* 58 (1967) 255–65.

PART II

The History of the Reverberations of Scripture

Pinchas Lapide

Exodus in the Jewish tradition

THE EARLIEST extant mention of Israel outside the Bible claims to be its last. An inscription of the Pharaoh Mernephta dated round about 1240 BC boasts laconically: 'Israel has been destroyed; its seed is no more.' But from our history we learn a different story:

> Now there arose a new king over Egypt ... And he said to his people, 'Behold, the people of Israel are too many and too mighty for us. Come, let us deal shrewdly with them, lest they multiply ...' Therefore they set taskmasters over them ... and made their lives bitter with hard service, in mortar and brick and in all kinds of work in the field ... Afterwards Moses and Aaron went to Pharaoh and said, 'Thus says the Lord, the God of Israel, "Let my people go ..."' But Pharaoh said, 'Who is the Lord, that I should heed his voice and let Israel go? I do not know the Lord, and moreover I will not let Israel go.' ... The same day Pharaoh commanded the taskmasters of the people and their foremen, '... Let heavier work be laid upon the men that they may labour at it and pay no regard to lying words.' (Exodus 1:8–14, 5:1–9)

Six months and ten plagues later things had finally reached this stage:

> And when in time to come your son asks you, 'What does this mean?' [of the feast of unleavened bread] you shall say to him, 'By strength of hand the Lord brought us out of Egypt, from the house of bondage.' (Exodus 13:14)

The rest every school-child knows, from Iceland to Chile, from Portugal to New Zealand: the Red Sea, the Egyptian army, Israel crossing dryshod where the Suez Canal is today, Pharaoh's horses and riders drowned in the waters, and Israel, freed from the heathen yoke, makes its way to Mount Sinai to become God's convenant community on earth. All this happened roughly 3,300 years ago—and yet this commemoration of the liberation of this people has lost nothing of its topicality. More than this: if the entire Hebrew Bible is a collection of dialogues between God and his covenent people, then this evergreen dialogue, which as a rehearsal of primeval experiences of God is the core of the entire Jewish tradition, becomes a process of training and educating people in the faith of their fathers.

For in the Passover, the Jewish feast of liberation and becoming a nation, it is above all the living God who is celebrated as the 'source of life', since what is involved in all his saving acts is life, experience, and survival.

All that survives of those Pharaohs is a few mummies, half a dozen pyramids that our forefathers had to build as slaves, and a handful of artefacts in museums. In contrast the remembrance of being led out of bondage which marks the start of Israel's real history of hope remains ever fresh and ever green.

1. A TURNING-POINT IN WORLD HISTORY

Why? Why has this exodus from the dawn of history not long since fallen prey to oblivion? It is because we Jews, unlike other religions, have *never separated the secular history of the world from the religious history of salvation.* Liberation has always been experienced in Israel as an historical event of this world which nevertheless is primarily and profoundly religious in its significance. For it is neither Moses nor Aaron who are the heroes of this drama but God, who reveals himself as the liberator of the weak and the oppressed. In this way this historical event reaches out far beyond itself, transcending both the individual case and the national boundaries of our people, in order to become for all victims of the inhuman subjugation and exploitation that is all too humanly common a continually renewed promise that in times of the profoundest distress serves as a beacon of hope.

Liberation, redemption and resurrection: these three fundamental ideas of all biblical theology are in their origins 'exodal' and find common expression in the Passover feast, to which the Hebrew Bible gives precedence over all other feasts (Exod. 12:2). This saving event, which represents the starting-point for the experience of Sinai and the subsequent colonisation of Canaan, is not merely to be perpetuated in the memory of the people but to go on living from generation to generation by being fully made present.

'It is *you* who were brought out of Egypt.' This is the core of the Jewish

Passover Ceremony—and thirty centuries of Jewish history have shown each single generation all too clearly the truth of this. The ritual of the Haggadah adds this reminder: 'For it was not one alone who rose against us to annihilate us, but in every generation there are those who rise against us to annihilate us. But the Holy One, blessed is He, ever saves us from their hand.' And this central theme is sounded more distinctively further on: 'This is on account of what the Lord did for me when I went forth from Egypt.'

This personalisation of the Exodus has turned out to be fully justified through a hundred generations. No Jewish child reaches the age of his barmitzvah (or her batmitzvah) without having felt and expressed the history of being brought out of Egypt as his or her own experience of the Passover.

This unique moment in the history of Israel that began by turning subjugated forced labourers into runaway slaves in order subsequently to forge them into the people of God in the harsh merciless desert has over three millennia become the *epitome of all liberation*. To quote simply one example, in 1776, when the United States had just gained their independence, Thomas Jefferson proposed as the national emblem of the young republic a representation of the children of Israel crossing the Red Sea, the moment of their transition from slavery to freedom. This was well justified, for already in the early Talmud the universal significance of the Exodus is emphasised. It was not only Israel that was brought out of Egypt, say the Rabbis in their interpretation of Exodus 12:38 with its mention of the 'mixed multitude', but with them the whole of mankind was brought out from the house of bondage.[1]

The Bible makes it clear that this slavery was not simply some form of feudal servitude but was *strikingly similar to the hell of the concentration camps* (Exod. 1:8–12, 5:6–20). The wearisome forced labour, the cruelty of the Egyptian officials, the psychosis of suspicion and hatred, the continuous terror, all of which served only to dehumanise people and to kill them like cattle—all this makes Egypt the predecessor of Auschwitz and, for our generation as for hardly any other in Israel's long history of suffering, makes the Exodus a contemporary reality.

But with the Exodus from the land of the Nile not only was a breach torn in the structure of the Egyptian tyranny, not only were the enslaved Hebrews liberated from their yoke, but a *turning-point was reached in world history*. The categorical imperative 'Let my people go' (Exod. 10:3) broke a spell under which mankind had suffered for too long. All values were completely overturned: the deified and Titan-like Pharaoh crumpled overnight to become the trembling father weeping at the bedside of his dying son—and finding out that he is no more than a man (Exod. 12:30). A horde of slaves and plebeians without rights recover the nobility of being made in the image of God. Two-legged animals become human beings. The Exodus event breaks the twin spell that all too long had turned some people into gods and had reduced others to cattle.

The breach made in godless tyranny by the Exodus creates the precondition of all Adam's children being equal by birth. Henceforth it opens up a solution for all human misery that no one will be able to block any longer—and until this day it remains the perpetual challenge to power. On the way to the Red Sea, as step by step liberation matured into certainty, differences between the runaway slaves gradually disappear: naked egotism breaks the limits of its own skin, differences fade away, and people discover in their fellows their neighbours.

2. PARTNERS

On the way to freedom *everyone became his or her fellow's neighbour*, and this applied to God too. In the book of Exodus we read (33:11) that 'the Lord used to speak to Moses face to face, as a man speaks to his friend'. And on Mount Sinai the gospel of the Hebrew proclamation is: 'I am the Lord your God, who brought you out of the land of Egypt, out of the house of bondage' (Exod. 20:2). The Exodus from Egypt—and, say the rabbis, that alone—gives God the right to say 'I' and to address man as 'you'. God's way to man leads through the squalor and misery of the fiery furnace to the revelation of Sinai, which gives the world its basic morality and the Exodus its original meaning.

'I am the Lord your God, who brought you forth out of the land of Egypt, that you should not be their slaves; and I have broken the bars of your yoke and made you walk erect' (Lev. 26:13). This saying provides the irrevocable warrant of the 'freedom of a Jewish human being', as Martin Luther might perhaps have put it and as Karl Barth indicated much later, in 1935. The great song of God-given freedom recognises only the creator of the world as lord and master, for as God himself tells us: 'They are my servants, whom I brought forth out of the land of Egypt; they shall not be sold as slaves' (Lev. 25:42). The rabbis elucidate this by saying: 'Therefore they must not become serfs or the servants of servants.'[2] Here is to be found the core of the Passover message that has inspired innumerable liberation movements, ideologies of emancipation and fighters for independence, from biblical times up until our own day.

3. PROTEST AND RESISTANCE

Since in the Jewish view of the world God and man are partners in the continuing saving work of ennobling the world, the *creature may even contradict its creator*: utter reproaches, raise protests—even to the verge of rebellion. 'But Abraham still stood before the Lord ... and said, "Wilt thou indeed destroy the righteous with the wicked? ... Far be that from thee! Shall not the Judge of all the earth do right?" ' (Gen. 18:22–25).

This trait of the fighter who dares to struggle even with God has been bequeathed by Jacob to the entire Jewish people along with its pugnacious name of Israel. The prophets are not slow to display their pugnacity: 'Lord, I would plead my case before thee,' Jeremiah tells God (Jer. 12:1–2). 'Why does the way of the wicked prosper? Why do all who are treacherous thrive? ... Thou art near in their mouth, and far from their heart.' Habakkuk reproached his creator (Hab. 1:2–3): 'O Lord, how long shall I cry for help, and thou wilt not hear? Or cry to thee "Violence!" and thou wilt not save? Why dost thou make me see wrongs and look upon trouble?' The psalmist is boldly rebellious (Ps. 44:23–24): 'Rouse thyself! Why sleepest thou, O Lord? Awake! Do not cast us off for ever! Why dost thou hide thy face? Why dost thou forget our affliction and oppression?' Job takes the same line in insisting on his integrity, even if his words appear to verge on blasphemy (Job 27:2–6): 'As God lives, who has taken away my right, and the Almighty, who has made my soul bitter; as long as my breath is in me ... I hold fast my righteousness, and will not let it go; my heart does not reproach me for any of my days.'

Very little imagination is needed to picture for oneself how Hebrews like this who wanted to call even God to account *dealt with their own flesh-and-blood rulers when these were corrupted by their power*. Thus the prophet Samuel publicly rebukes King Saul: 'You have done foolishly ... Why did you swoop on the spoil, and do what was evil in the sight of the Lord? ... Because you have rejected the word of the Lord, he has also rejected you from being king' (1 Sam. 13:13, 15:19, 23). Similarly Elijah damns King Ahab as a thief and a murderer, while the prophet Nathan does not hesitate to denounce King David himself in front of his court: 'You are the man. Thus says the Lord, ... "Why have you despised the word of the Lord, to do what is evil in his sight? You have smitten Uriah the Hittite with the sword, and have taken his wife to be your wife, and have slain him with the sword of the Ammonites." ' (2 Sam. 12:7, 9).

These were not pious Sunday sermons but theological and political declarations of war that in every case involved a risk to life—originally for the accusers themselves but subsequently for the kings of Israel, whose rule always remained subject to the criticism of the prophets.

As far as *foreign domination* was concerned, or the heathen yoke, as the Pharisees called it in contrast to the heavenly yoke of the Torah, the urge to freedom that had its origins in the Exodus was immeasurably stronger. It resounds again and again in prophecy: 'I have broken your fetters so that you may become my servants, says the Lord; you shall not be the servants of my servants' (Sifra on Lev. 25:42). Hence during the last three centuries of the era of the Second Temple there were no fewer than 62 Jewish revolts, rebellions, attempts at revolution and resistance movements. Most of these had their origin in Galilee and often fully occupied between two and four whole Roman legions. This went on until the last two Jewish wars when the insignificant fringe province of Judaea succeeded in challenging the best fighting forces of the Roman Empire—until Judaea collapsed.

But not even the national catastrophe of the 70s of the first century could put an end to the *unquenchable longing for that freedom that God himself had guaranteed in Holy Writ*. If defeat, banishment and the destruction of the Temple were not accepted, if between 115 and 117 there was the Jewish revolt against the emperor Trajan, and despite the most savage repression the Bar Kochba rebellion broke out fifteen years later and led to Jewish freedom flaring up again for three years; if in Galilee Jews once again took up arms against Constantine in 351; if as late as 614, more than half a millennium after the laying waste of the whole of Judaea, a joint rebellion of Jewish fighters and Persians could break out—then all these desperate struggles express not only one small people's urgent need for freedom but are also sparks of a *Messianic fire* that sees freedom as a pre-condition for redemption, a fire that had its origin in God's liberation theology in the Exodus and that no human hand as yet has been able to quench.

It is no wonder that *most freedom movements inside and outside the churches*, from the Cathars of Provence to the Waldensians of northern Italy, the Hussites of Bohemia, the Puritans and the Methodists in England, and the Pilgrim Fathers who built their promised land in America, have sought and have also found their inspiration, their vocabulary of salvation and their legitimation in the Bible of the Jews. In this way we find themes and phrases from the second book of Moses not only in the liturgies of the churches but also in the political slogans and songs of oppressed peoples from the Blacks of Mississippi to the Maoris of New Zealand, from the Zulus of South Africa to the Blacks of Jamaica, from the Indians of Camillo Torres in Colombia to the Mineros of Bolivia, not to forget the independent Black Churches of contemporary Zimbabwe.

Thus in his last speech, in Memphis in April 1968, Martin Luther King, the champion of Black emancipation in the United States, said: 'I do not know what will happen now. But fundamentally it does not make any difference to me ... For I have ascended Mount Nebo and I have seen the promised land. ... It may be that I shall not make it, but you should know that we as the people of God will come into the promised land. I do not fear any man, for my eyes have seen the glory of the fulfilled promise.'

The depth to which the Exodus has bitten into people's consciousness can be heard from what the former general secretary of the World Council of Churches, Dr Phillip Potter, said when some years ago in Geneva he was briefing the WCC's Central Committee on Nairobi: 'While in Uppsala we found ourselves in an Exodus atmosphere and considered the liberating encounter with God's plan of salvation without hesitation, in Nairobi we had the feeling of finding ourselves in the desert.' In this situation Dr Potter could of course give his gloomy diagnosis a perspective full of promise, for in God's economy the desert is the only possible pilgrim path for those who have accepted God's promise. It was in the desert that God concluded his covenant with the people of Israel.

4. THREE THEMES

Three themes or fundamental ideas of universal human validity are contained in the experience of the Exodus.

The biblical *demythologisation of the idols of the ancient world*, with all their sphinxes, ibises, Osiris and Horus, whose incarnation the Pharaoh was, meant that the 'gods' of the idol-worshippers were defeated and stripped of their power. After the downfall of the gods in the Exodus, God enters the field of history. The eternal, never-ending dialogue between creator and creature begins neither with moral sermons nor with theological speculations but with the insight that the creator is a God of freedom: 'I have broken the bars of your yoke and made you walk erect,' God says to his people (Lev. 26:13) who with their newly discovered human dignity are promoted to be God's partner in dialogue. *Exodus and liberation were actual social and political events*: an emancipation of body and soul as actual as the future redemption foreshadowed in the Exodus Passover that Judaism expects and hopes for. The Messianic last days are not something Israel sees in allegorical or spiritual terms but as something decidedly physical and not just ethical, earthly and human and not just divine, precisely in accordance with the unequivocal testimony of all biblical experiences of God.

Among the innumerable suggestions and possible implementations that the Exodus offers contemporary emancipators and teachers, three should be mentioned briefly.

First, 'the more they [the people of Israel] were oppressed, the more they multiplied and the more they spread abroad' (Exod. 1:12). This historical *connection between Israel's persecutions, its power of suffering, and its persistence through trust in God* that has culminated in the present-day return of the Jews to the land of their fathers, offers a tactical pointer not just for

Israel's contemporary history but also as an optimistic indicator for every as yet unliberated nation everywhere.

Secondly, 'and Moses said to the people, "Fear not, stand firm, and see the salvation of the Lord, which he will work for you today ... The Lord will fight for you, and you have only to be still." ' The Lord said to Moses, 'Why do you cry to me? Tell the people of Israel to go forward' (Exod. 14:13–15). This *contrast between Moses' passivity that trusts in God and God's desire for men and women to work with him* is a well-known theme in the Talmud,[3] which uses didactic examples and parables to corroborate the biblical truism that faith without works is just as fruitless as hope without deeds.

The third significance of the Exodus story is perhaps the most profound but at the same time the most difficult of the lessons taught us by God's evergreen word. With cruel realism the Bible tells us that year after year of wandering in the desert the cry of the people was never silenced: 'We want to go back to Egypt.' The *bread of freedom was hard and dry*, unlike the secure chains and the fare of that distant labour camp on the Nile. In the course of time the fleshpots of Egypt became richer and richer, the meagre manna more and more miserable; looking back slavery seemed ever more endurable and the desert ever more barren. It did not do Moses any good that he assured the people that manna would rain down from heaven every morning; it should not however be kept, not even for a single night. To rely so completely on God, blindly and without any loopholes or emergency exit, seemed to runaway slaves far too sinister. And so many began to doubt the meaning of freedom: wandering around in the desert seemed pointless, so too did the distant invisible goal. It was even more pointless to build on being dependent on an invisible God who appeared ever more puny and powerless the stronger fear grew for life itself. It did not help them, for their understanding of God was as puny as they were themselves.

And so arose the harsh judgment that has lost nothing of its topicality today. For forty years the mixed multitude of helots and serfs had to wait in the desert, *until they and their weak slave mentality disappeared into the sand* so that their free-born desert sons and daughters could conquer the land of freedom and take it into possession. *Exodus from slavery is one goal, entry into freedom is the second.* To reach it needs trust and courage and obedience, since according to the rabbis it is only the person who takes the yoke of heaven on himself or herself who is truly free. The way out of slavery leads one by three stages: through the harsh hungry desert, then the giving of the law on Mount Sinai, and only then the taking of Canaan. That is the liberation theology the Bible teaches us.

To drum this fundamental aspect of salvation properly into the minds of the people of Israel the Talmud uses a Hebrew play on words that has not lost its relevance. Commenting on Exodus's statement after Moses had come down from Sinai (Exod. 32:16), 'And the tables were the work of God, and the writing was the writing of God, graven upon the tables,' the rabbis said one should read not 'graven' but 'free' (*cherut* instead of *charut*), since there is no free man beyond him who voluntarily bows to the yoke of the kingdom of heaven.[4] To put it another way, freedom without fear of God is anarchy, just as liberation without self-discipline must mean becoming the slave of every animal instinct.

The Exodus from Egypt belongs among humankind's core experiences that Israel was chosen to exemplify for the community of nations. Since that Exodus all human power and force comes up against a divine boundary. For a broad way leads out of all deserts of oppression, all houses of bondage and man's inhumanity—through the divided waters of the Red Sea to the revelation of Mount Sinai and from there to Canaan, the eternal land of the freedom promised by God.

Translated by Robert Nowell

Notes

1. Exodus Rabba 18.
2. See Lev. 25:42.
3. Mechilta on Exodus 14:13 and Sota 37a, where we read: 'At that hour Moses spent a long time in prayer, and the Holy One, blessed be He, said to him: "My beloved children are drowning in the sea—and you waste time before me in lengthy prayer?" ' See also Sanh 39b.
4. Tanchuma B. Ki Tissa 12; Exodus Rabba 32; Numbers Rabba 16.

John Newton

Analysis of Programmatic Texts of Exodus Movements

WHEN ISRAEL came out of Egypt, she experienced more than liberation from bondage, at the hands of her out-of-Egypt-bringing-God. She was drawn into a new stream of history as a pilgrim people. She was called to cross not only physical barriers—the Red Sea, the Sinai Desert—but also *new frontiers of mind and spirit*. Even after she had reached Canaan, the land of promise, her journey, in the deepest sense, was not over. Indeed, it may be said to have scarcely begun. Always she would be called to travel through history in obedience to her covenant God, and in quest of his promises.

1. HISTORICAL MIGRATIONS

The *many Exodus movements in Christian history* have drawn rich inspiration from the archetypal event and meanings of the Exodus as: call, liberation, testing, journeying and attainment of new beginnings in a land of promise. Many of these movements were inspired by a theology of hope and promise, which included a fresh beginning in a new place, where men would be free to create a new form of Church and society. Such, for example, was the movement of emigration among seventeenth-century Puritans, who sought to leave the 'Egypt' or 'Babylon' of old England, for the Canaan of New England in America. The pioneer colonists were not all inspired by religious motives, it is true. Some saw America as Utopia, El Dorado, or another Eden, demi-Paradise. Yet there were many who saw it as another Canaan, if not a New Jerusalem, and who sailed westward in the spirit of Exodus, convinced that they were called and chosen of God to inherit the promises, in a good land and a large.

Yet though the Exodus from England to North America brought freedom to the Puritan emigrants, they had first to pass through the *wilderness*. Cotton Mather, in his classic history of the New England churches, *Magnalia Christi Americana* (1702), recalled Luther's similitude of the Church as, 'a silly poor maid, sitting in a wilderness, compassed about with hungry lions, wolves, boars and bears, and all manner of cruel and hurtful beasts'. He saw 'that picture of the Church exemplified in the story of New-England' and affirmed that, 'the people of the Lord Jesus Christ, "led into the wilderness" of New-England, have not only met with a continual temptation of the devil there— the wilderness having always had serpents in it—but also they have had, in almost every lustre of years, a new assault of extraordinary temptation upon them; a more than common "hour and power of darkness" ' (Mather *Magnalia* edn., 1853, II pp. 499–500). The 'wilderness' here has a dual reference. It is the wilderness of temptation, in which Jesus fought against Satan's wiles and overcame. At the same time the reference to 'the serpents' links the wilderness experience to the Exodus (see Deuteronomy 8:15; Numbers 21:5–9).

2. AN EXODUS WITHOUT MIGRATION

On the other hand, some exodus movements do not centre on a physical migration to a new land or continent. They are committed rather to a programme of *consciousness-raising and an agenda of social and political change*. Such movements use powerfully the language of Exodus, as did *Dr Martin Luther King* in his leadership of the Civil Rights movement of the Negroes of the Southern States of America. Preaching in the cathedral of St John the Divine, New York, on 17 May 1956, he reminded his congregation that they met on the second anniversary of the momentous decision of the United States Supreme Court that segregated schooling was unconstitutional and must cease. He took his text from Exodus 14:30 ('And Israel saw the Egyptians dead upon the seashore'), and drove home the decisiveness of that historic judgment. Comparing the Negro struggle to the Hebrews' escape from Egyptian slavery, he proclaimed: 'Today we are witnessing a massive change. A world-shaking decree by the nine Justices of the United States Supreme court opened the Red Sea, and the forces of justice are crossing to the other side ... looking back we see the forces of segregation dying on the seashore.' This comparison brings out the grotesque disparity between the might of 'the forces of segregation', buttressed by economic power, political influence, and the rooted prejudice of generations; and the puny material resources of the down-trodden Negro people, on whom second-class citizenship had been imposed as a way of life. Yet as Pharaoh's chariots and horsemen could not prevent the Israelites crossing over to freedom and safety, neither could the might of 'the forces of segregation' hold back Luther King's people from the freedom which was their due. There is the same sense of wonder here as in the Book of Exodus, and the same profound acknowledgment that the deliverance is a mighty act of God, the God of justice and mercy.

Martin Luther King, in calling up the archetypal image of the Red Sea crossing from bondage to liberation, was drawing on the ancestral sources of Negro spirituality. The slaves of the Southern plantations had expressed their faith and longing for freedom in their own version of the Psalms of Lamentation—the *Spirituals*. As protest songs, hymns of faith, appeals to God's mercy, the Spirituals return continually to the themes of the Exodus deliverance. So, in 'Go down, Moses', for example, the slaves sang:

> Israel was in Egypt's land,
> Let my people go,
> Oppress'd so hard they could not stand,
> Let my people go.
> Go down, Moses, way down in Egypt's land,
> Tell ole Pharoh, to let my people go.

After the Red Sea crossing, and the long years of wandering in the desert, the Israelites at last entered Canaan, the land of promise. The Negroes of the South use the same haunting imagery to express their hope of heaven:

> Deep river, my home is over Jordan,
> Deep river, I want to cross over into camp-ground.
> Oh, don't you want to go to that gospel feast,
> That promis'd land where all is at peace?
> Oh deep river, Lord,
> I want to cross into camp-ground.

Another Spiritual, dealing with the siege and sack of Jericho, ('And the walls came tumblin' down'), reminds us of the darker, shadow side of the Exodus events, as these culminated in the conquest and occupation of Canaan. Joshua 6:20–21 describes the taking of Jericho by the Israelites and the merciless treatment of the inhabitants, who are systematically 'devoted to destruction' so that Israel may dispossess them: 'Then they utterly destroyed all in the city, both men and women, young and old, oxen, sheep, and asses, with the edge of the sword' (R.S.V.).

3. CONQUEST RATHER THAN CONVERSION

This biblical precedent has proved, at various turning-points in Christian history, *quite disastrous as a paradigm for followers of Christ* who saw themselves as called and elected to go in and possess a 'Promised Land' at the expense of the 'Canaanites' already there. The South African historian, van Jaarsveld, for instance, sums up the impact of the Puritan settlement of North America on the Red Indian tribes who were indigenous to the land: 'Calvinists who settled in North America believed that they were God's chosen people whose footsteps had been directed to the land of Canaan. This belief was decisive in so far as it led to the near-extinction of the redskin and the preservation of the whites'. (F. A. van Jaarsveld *The Afrikaners' Interpretation of South African History* Johannesburg 1962 p. 5).

Among the many motives—religious, political, economic—which inspired the seventeenth-century Puritan colonisation of America, the conversion of the Red Indians certainly bulked large in the minds of those in England who sponsored the settlement. These men—merchants, lawyers, politicians—were critical of the pioneers for not more actively pursuing the original ideal of evangelising the Red Man. Schneider is clear that 'In general the New Englanders took the attitude that the Indians were not fit subjects for the Kingdom of God ... John Cotton' (a leading minister of Boston, Massachusetts) 'even found a passage in the Scriptures indicating that it was not the will of God that the Indians should be converted until certain other things had first taken place' (H. W. Schneider *The Puritan Mind* University of Michigan 1958 p. 39). These other things were the defeat of Antichrist and the large-scale conversion of the Jews. Meanwhile, conquest rather than conversion remained the primary aim, and the Revd Thomas Shepard of Cambridge, Massachusetts, who was by no means a vindictive character, could describe the massacre of the Pequot tribe as a 'divine slaughter by the hand of the English'. William Haller, another Puritan specialist, confirms this general picture: 'From one point of view they (*sc.* the Red Indians) were at best Canaanites or at worst imps of the evil one with no rights that the chosen people were bound to respect' (W. Haller *Liberty and Reformation in the Puritan Revolution* Columbia 1963 p. 154).

There were, indeed, some *magnificent exceptions* to this overall outlook. Roger Williams of Providence, Rhode Island, a pioneer of religious toleration and racial liberalism, was one such. William Penn and the Quakers of Pennsylvania preached and practised peace towards the Indians. The Revd John Eliot, who translated the Bible into Algonquin and became the outstanding 'Apostle to the Red Indians', was strong in their defence. But these were exceptions, and shone as lights in a dark world.

4. THE GREAT TREK OF THE BOERS

We may see a similar pattern of exodus-wandering-conquest-settlement, in the history of another significant group of Calvinists—the *Voortrekkers of South Africa*, the Boers who embarked on the Great Trek north from the Cape in 1836–38. Van Jaarsveld brings out well the way in which the Afrikaners readily identified themselves with the Exodus experience of Israel: '... the way of life of the Boers was similar to that of Israel of old ... One has to appreciate the loneliness, the vast expanses of the veld, the trek into the unknown with all their possessions and livestock, the patriarchal nature of family relationships and of forms of government, the starry firmament by night and the scorching sun by day and the dangers of wild beasts and barbarians that threatened their existence from day to day. For the Afrikaners the parallel with the chosen of the Lord grew into a form of mystecism (*sic*); by their sufferings in fulfilling God's calling they would be purified.' (Van Jaarsveld *op. cit.*, p. 10). The very terminology of the Voortrekkers reveals the direct influence of the Old Testament, which seemed so close to them in their world of bush and veld. 'Maritz spoke in 1837 of the new land "overflowing with milk and honey"; they appointed "Judges" to rule over them; some of them wished to call Natal "New Eden"; Sunday was "the day of the Sabbath"; their trek was a wandering in "the desert"; before Blood River (*sc.* the site of their great battle with the Zulus) they entered into "a compact" with God, while references to "promised land", "the God of our fathers" and the place name "The River Nile" too show how literally they applied the words of the Old Testament. It is recorded that many of Potgieter's group of Trekkers believed that they were a chosen people of God journeying to the land of Canaan with their leader as a second Moses' (Van Jaarsveld *op. cit.*). After the Great Trek, the Boers increasingly hardened in their attitude to the Black people, whom they saw as 'Naatsies', the nations without the Law, Canaanites or Philistines. When Commandant P. E. Scholtz had subdued the Zulu chief Sechele in the 1850s, he declared that he had acted in this matter in strict accordance with the divine law that had been entrusted to Joshua.

5. THE GREAT JOURNEY OF THE MORMONS

In the final example of an exodus movement which falls to be considered here, there was, by contrast, no harsh treatment of the people of the land. This movement, way out on the sectarian fringe of Christendom, was the great journey of the *Mormons*, or The Church of Jesus Christ of Latter-Day Saints, from Illinois to Utah in 1847. Joseph Smith, the Mormon founder, had led his people to Illinois, their 'Land of Zion', where they established a settlement at Nauvoo, on the eastern bank of the Mississippi. When Smith was killed by a lynch-mob in 1844, and as opposition to the Mormons' doctrines and way of life mounted, however, they decided to decamp to the far West of the continent. The 1,500-mile journey, undertaken in a series of waggon-trains, was formidably difficult. It involved the emigrants in a long saga of hunger, exhaustion, sickness, harsh labour, danger from wild beasts, and the continual threat of Indian attacks.

Clearly, a powerful incentive and a strong leader were both needed to inspire the stubborn determination to accomplish what has been called 'The Mormon Hegira', but which is better described as the Mormon Exodus. Incentive and leader came together in the person of Brigham Young, polygamist, astute business man, and prophetic leader of the 'Latter-Day Saints'. Young summoned the Mormon pioneers to take the trail to the West, in marching orders which he proclaimed as a direct revelation from God. His language throughout is reminiscent of the Book of Exodus, and assumes the complete identification of the Mormons with the Israel of God, as the following extract illustrates: 'The Word and Will of the Lord, given through President Brigham Young, at the Winter Quarters of the Camp of Israel, Omaha Nation, West Bank of the Missouri River, near Council Bluffs, 14 January 1847. The Word and will of the Lord concerning the Camp of Israel in their journeyings to the West; let all the people of the Church of Jesus Christ of Latter-Day Saints ... be organised into companies, with a covenant and promise to keep all the commandments and statutes of the Lord our God ... let every man use his influence and property to remove this people to the place where the Lord shall locate a Stake of Zion.'

This great trek of the Mormons, which involved crossing the Great Plains and the formidable barrier of the Rocky Mountains, had an heroic dimension to it. All Young's skill as organiser was required by the sheer logistics of the operation. He had also to provide leadership and encouragement to followers who, like old Israel, were apt to 'murmur' and complain when the going became hard. It is scarcely surprising that a recent life of the Mormon leader should be entitled *Brigham Young: American Moses* (by Leonard J. Arrington, New York 1985). On Sunday 25 April 1847, having with difficulty forded a tributary of the River Platte, they held a service of worship at which Brigham Young referred to complaints in the camp, in terms which recall Exodus 16:2–3, where '... the whole congregation of the people of Israel murmured against Moses and Aaron in the wilderness, and said to them, "Would that we had died by the hand of the Lord in the land of Egypt ... when we sat by the fleshpots and ate bread to the full; for you have brought us out into this wilderness to kill this whole assembly with hunger" '. Young in his discourse singled out one of the leading complainants against 'Moses' ' leadership, with the sarcastic suggestion that, 'anyone who wants to murmur, go to Henry G. Sherwood, who will do the business for them'.

Again, to Mormon understanding, the miracle of the manna, of bread in the desert, was also repeated in their own exodus. At the crossing of the River Platte, they used their one leather boat to ferry the baggage of a group of non-Mormons emigrating westward along the Oregon Trail. The latter paid the Mormons for their help in flour, meal, and bacon, just as their own supplies were failing. Woodruff, a Mormon leader, wrote: 'It looked as much of a miracle to me, to see our flour and meal bags replenished in the midst of the Black Hills as it did to have the Children of Israel fed with manna in the wilderness.'

By the 1850s, they were well established in Utah, and Young, preaching in the Old Salt Lake Tabernacle, (which itself spoke of the Exodus 'Tent of Meeting'), could claim that the Mormon Exodus was even more remarkable than its biblical prototype: 'The miracles wrought in the days of Moses for the deliverance of the children of Israel from Egyptian bondage as they are recorded in the Old Testament, appear to be wonderful displays of the power of God ... The children of Israel ... were brought out of Egypt ... to inherit a land flowing with milk and honey; we have assembled in these distant valleys for the trial of our faith. They were delivered out of a dreadful bondage, leaving none behind; we have willingly ... left ... friends, parents, companions, etc., behind. ...'

These examples of exodus movements, drawn from Church History, may suggest the *abiding power of the Exodus as a paradigm of God's dealings with his people*. The sequence of: election, promise, call, liberation, testing on the long trek, and final arrival at the land of promise, has shown ample power to strengthen men and women to face privation and danger with great determination and resilience. The shadow side of Exodus, in the ill-treatment and expropriation of the 'Canaanites' or 'Gentiles', is, however, a warning that the Exodus pattern, construed in literalist Old Testament terms, has exacted a heavy toll in human suffering. Of the examples surveyed here, only Martin Luther King's non-violent campaign for Negro rights and dignity, and for reconciliation of Black and White, points unambiguously to what is for Christians *the* Exodus, the 'Exodus' which Jesus, by his death and resurrection, 'was to accomplish at Jerusalem' (Luke 9:31).

Anton Weiler

The Experience of Communities of Religious Refugees

1. EXODUS COMMUNITIES

'EXODUS COMMUNITIES'—this is the collective name that three millenaristic groups of people who *left their ordinary environment* in order to wait in a special place for the coming of the Lord gave themselves.[1] The first were the 'Grusinic separatists', a group of pietists from Wurtemberg in Germany who, because of liturgical renewals about 1843 that displeased them, went to Grusia in Georgia, with the intention of going on from there to Palestine. Their plan did not succeed. The second were the 'Amenic community' (see Isa. 65:16). Their leader was Israel Pick from Bohemia (1824?–59), whose intention was to found a Mosaic-Christian church with its centre in Jerusalem. This initiative also came to nothing. The third of these groups was the free church community that came about at the instigation of Pastor Samuel Gottfried Clöter from Illenschwang (1823–94) as the *Deutsche Auszugsgemeinde* in 1878 in Stuttgart, with the intention of fleeing to transcaucasian Russia in order to escape from the misery of the imminent rule of the Antichrist.

All three were concerned with settlements elsewhere and, in a sectarian spirit, made attempts which resulted in their having very similar adventures. According to Moritz Busch, writing at the end of the nineteenth century, they were 'uneducated men with a need for religion who left the cultural environment in which they had grown up and went to the loneliness of settlements in the forests, steppes or mountains where they were led to dream, muse and contemplate and therefore indulged in the same strange fantasies.

63

and became almost the same wonderful saints, whether they built their homes in the far West or the far East'.[2]

Forming conventicles leads again and again to the same problems of conflicts over authority, of simple preachers who call themselves and interpret the Bible in a fundamentalist way and of a continuous criticism of the teaching and behaviour of all members of the community.

2. OLD LUTHERAN REFUGEES

Comparable results have been produced by *modern historical research.* David Gerber[3] has described the exodus of Lutherans which was the consequence of the decision made by King Frederick William III of Prussia to achieve a fusion of the Reformed, the Calvinist and the Lutheran churches in his territory (1817). Two thousand five hundred Prussian Christians refused to accept the plan for unity, regarding it as a violation of their consciences, and emigrated under the leadership of their Old Lutheran preachers. In August to September 1838, six hundred Lutherans sailed under the leadership of a preacher, August Kavel, to Australia. In June to July 1839, six ships set sail for the United States with twelve hundred Lutherans led by Johann Grabau. Gerber has vividly described the problems associated with emigration because of faith. They can be summarised as problems of uprooting and resettlement, isolation and estrangement from one's own history and from the family and community in which one grew up and the trauma of a parting that was not wanted, unexpected and humiliating. He has also described the problems of self-conscious and barely ideologically motivated communities prepared to make sacrifices and consisting of large families and individuals who, driven into exile, had to take into account the need to establish new communal bonds in a strange country. The mixed social composition of these groups and the differences between rich and poor and between independent masters and dependent workers were subjected to the conservative attitude towards faith that the preachers insisted on as an obligatory element.

In the *United States,* for example, Grabau had a strictly confessionalistic approach towards his group, constantly urging them to preserve the pure doctrine of the sixteenth and seventeenth centuries and, because there was no State authority that promoted forms of faith, the preacher had the responsibility to do this. Gerber expresses this situation of conflict in the following way: 'It was the experience of the Old Lutheran exodus and then of American society and culture which sharpened his views and made them manifest and central in his dealings with others.'[4] The Old Lutherans despaired of American culture and its fundamental freedom of thought and in reaction cultivated their own sectarian identity by clinging to their own language, schools and seminaries and to their own German architecture. Their purity of doctrine led them to cultural isolation and to the introduction of a strict organisation and control in the Buffalo Synod. Grabau followed the path of public warnings and inquisitions, finally excluding dissident believers from the group. This went on until the congregation ultimately turned against him.

The same developments took place in *Australia* in very different circumstances. The emigrants did not encounter any fixed social system that challenged their faith. There were no people who were recognisably hostile. The problem was rather: How could a new social order be established in the wilderness, in other words, in a completely disorientating context that was full of material problems. Isolation and a great distance from their home country coupled with the certainty that it was impossible to return home formed a firm bond between these little settlements modelled on the Prussian village. A desire to preserve the earlier culture had to compete with millenaristic expectations and this led to schisms even within the same family. The Church had therefore to accept the role of political organisation and more and more rules were formulated by Kavel in order to preserve cohesion within the disenchanted group.

Gerber comes to very much the same conclusion as Busch did a hundred years ago. He has this to say about the religious refugee communities in the United States and Australia: 'Though the circumstances varied, in neither society were the exiles able to sustain the unity and clarity of purpose and belief they had gained under the reign of repression and persecution. In the end, however, their problems were the consequence not merely of the alleviation, through flight, of harsh conditions imposed by State authorities, but also, in the fullest sense, of the brittleness of their own beliefs and institutions under the impact of severe testing in new, freer environments. This, then, was the tragedy of their experience, a tragedy not unlike that experienced by other exiled religious communities: the self-determination they gambled for in leaving their place of oppression proved a basis for the undoing of the institutions and beliefs they had sought, in the first place, to defend.'[5]

3. THE FIRST DECADES OF THE AMERICAN PURITANS

Gerber then refers in an accompanying note to the American Puritans, who were faced with the same dilemma.[6] Study of American Puritanism has produced a firmly based image of the real nature of the English refugee communities in the New World.[7] Their experience is our most important source for a true understanding of the adventures and gradual decline of the exodus communities and for this reason it is valuable to describe them in greater detail here.

(a) The Pilgrim Fathers

The story begins with the Pilgrim Fathers, as the English Puritans called themselves. These Pilgrims arrived in New England in 1620 as the first colonists there. They have to be seen against the background of the struggle of the English Puritans against the established Church and the existing authority.[8] In the religious climate of the end of the sixteenth and the beginning of the seventeenth centuries, opposition to and separation from the Church of England was an expression of *conservative Calvinism*. The Puritans took as their points of departure in doctrine the predestination of the elect, the right of individuals to read and interpret Scripture for themselves and the need for the Church to be rooted in Scripture alone. The separatists wanted to live for God alone and according to his decrees and in accordance with their consciences and their conception of religion. The Church of England was, however, for a man like John Robinson, the pastor of the separated community that had emigrated to Leiden, and according to his *Justification of the Separation from the Church of England* (1610), not structured in accordance with the model of the New Testament Church.

How, then, should a true Church be structured? It had to consist of people who made a voluntary confession of faith and who separated themselves from the world in a covenant with God that was similar to God's covenant with Abraham. No one could be made a member of the Church simply by being subject to the King of England. Robinson was convinced that, in matters of faith and morals, it was a question of *personal responsibility* in the realisation of a Christian way of life. Two or three such people who voluntarily made a confession of faith—and were not forced to make it by the law or their circumstances of life—could together form a Church. 'This we hold and affirm, that a company consisting though but of two or three, separated from the world ... and gathered into the name of Christ by a covenant made to walk in all the ways of God known unto them, is a church and so hath the whole power of Christ.'[9]

The authority for the government of the Church was therefore invested not in a presbyterate, a bishop or an archbishop, but in the *members of the congregation*. And, on the basis of this idea of the complete autonomy of the local congregation, these men withdrew from the world and also from the existing Church of the Anglican unity. The Puritans who remained in the Church certainly resisted the vestments, the ceremonies and the vanities of the bishops and the liturgical forms of worship, but they continued to recognise the Church of England as a Christian community. The separatists, on the other hand, drew the ultimate conclusion from their individual status as believers and went off as Pilgrims in search of the possibility of bringing people together into a Church that would correspond to the standards of the Gospel and the models provided by the early history of the Church. They were to try to reactualise the history of the Church and indeed the history of Israel as the people of the covenant.

Even as a twelve year old boy, *William Bradford* (1590–1657),[10] who was born in Austerfield in Yorkshire, was an avid reader of the Bible. He joined the separatists who met in the home of William Brewster in Scrooby. This community fled with their preacher, John Robinson, to Amsterdam in 1609 and later moved to Leiden in Holland. Bradford was the leader of the emigration to New England in 1621 and was elected as governor of the Plymouth Colony in April 1621, an office that he held for thirty years. In the two decades between 1630 and 1650, he wrote his history of the *Plymouth Plantation*, in which he described how the believers, illuminated by the Word of God, had become conscious of their sins and had tried to reform their lives and their religious experience. They abominated the ceremonies and feasts that the Anglican Church had retained from its Roman past and regarded the worldly power of the Anglican prelates over their dependent subjects as conflicting with the freedom of the Gospel. They had finally shaken off the yoke of anti-Christian slavery as the Jewish people had done in Egypt and had come together as the free people of God to form a 'church estate by a covenant of the Lord'.

This new people of the covenant was persecuted by the official Church and by those in authority. They were thrown into prison, their houses were seized and they were watched day and night. Living under such pressure, they decided, for the sake of the purity of faith, to emigrate to the Netherlands, where it was possible to practise one's religion in freedom. Bradford freely admits than an exodus made for the sake of a pure conscience can demand a great deal from people. The decision to leave a simple but safe existence in the old English system for the sake of one's conscience must have been a very hard one.

The definitive exodus to America, where they hoped to experience God's commandments in purity within the framework of a Church and social order that was in accordance with the precepts of the Bible, took them even further away from home. When they arrived there, all that they found was a wilderness beyond an unknown coast, full of wild animals and wild people. They were not able to climb Mount Pisgah like the scouts of the people of Israel and see the Promised Land ahead of them. They could, however, and did accept the wilderness as a place given to them by God where they could build his city on the mountain and sing Psalm 107.

In God's name they also joined in a mutual agreement. The deed of 11 November 1620 sets out in very clear language how the members of the crew regarded their settlement. Even before they went ashore, the model of a secular political community living in the sight of God was confirmed.

(b) The Great Migration

The Plymouth Colony of 1620 was the work of a little group of emigrants on the coast of Massachusetts, but the Pilgrim Fathers soon had company when a second initiative at colonisation, beginning with the Massachusetts Bay Company, was undertaken. The leaders of this second group were *rich and prominent Puritans who had decided in secret to introduce the Congregational model into New England.* As soon as they had been given a royal charter for the establishment and managerial setting up of a colony in 1629, the great migration could begin.

The fleet of the 'Great Migration' arrived in 1630 under the leadership of *John Winthrop* (1588–1649).[11] This Justice of the Peace, whose grandfather had acquired Groton Manor in Norfolk in 1544 at the time of the dissolution of the Catholic monasteries, but who had lost his function in 1629 when King Charles dissolved Parliament, regarded himself as the Moses and the leader of a new and even more important exodus. Because of the decline of religion in England, Christ, he believed, wanted to liberate his people from their long slavery under presumptuous princes of the Church and to found a new heaven and a new earth, new churches and a new commonwealth. Purity in religion was the motivating force behind the initiative undertaken by these men who aimed to found their own Church of visible saints, little groups electing their own elders and deriving their authority directly from Christ. The separation of these voluntary exiles and especially of the leader, John Winthrop, and the ministers from their friends and relatives has been described by Edward Johnson (1598–1672) in his *Wonder Working Providence of Sion's Savior* (1654).[12] The rupture brought about by this exodus in the bonds of blood-relationships and natural affection between people can be heard in the author's words, together with the firm plan to found only pure churches of saints.

On the deck of the flagship of the great fleet, the Arabella, in the middle of the Atlantic Ocean, John Winthrop described the essence of the social ideal of the new community in a lay sermon. This document, which is regarded as fundamental for an understanding of the 'Puritan mind', has been given, in Perry Miller's edition, the title: 'A Model of Christian Love (of Neighbour)'[13] The text is written in the idiom of the Old Testament and of the ideas current in jurisprudence at the time, but it is also equally in the tradition of late medieval nominalistic theology and the Protestantism of Martin Bucer. The mode of expression of these 'Congregational Puritans' has its centre in their *concept of the covenant*. The Church community is seen as a covenant of saints with God and the community of people is seen as a social covenant of Church members who aim to make the biblical precepts and rules of behaviour literally valid. Both are regarded as the concrete expression of the covenant between God and Christians, as that covenant was foreshadowed in the covenant between Yahweh and the Hebrews. This idea of the covenant expresses the election and the perseverance in faith of the saints, but it also expresses God's faithfulness to his people and in particular to the New Englanders, who had followed his call to purity to the extent of making a new beginning in the wilderness.

Winthrop closed his address with the encouragement that Moses gave to the people in his last discourse (Deut. 30). He was full of hope, but his Journal reveals how he had, as the governor of the colony and under pressure from the ministers, *to govern the colony in a hard manner*. The covenant idea did not point to the need to establish a democracy or to aim at equality among individuals. The people had been brought together on God's terms, not in a free association, but only with the freedom to do what God commanded them to do through their leaders. That meant what magistrates such as John Winthrop, educated pastors such as John Cotton, the teacher of the Boston Church, and Thomas Hooker, the minister of Newton, regarded as good, just and honourable.[14] For his new settlement in Connecticut in 1636, Hooker outlined a series of positive laws giving form to the ideal Christian community.

The Massachusetts colony accepted an all-embracing code of law in 1648 in the so-called *Book of General Laws*, which had the Bible as an important point of departure, but in which a significant part was played by the traditional English practice of Common Law in the formulation of legal statutes. English exiles, who had been living in Geneva during the reign of Mary Stuart, had become acquainted in that city with a legal system that had derived a great deal from the Bible and, under the influence of Calvinism, the eighteenth chapter of Leviticus had been introduced as a positive law into Scotland. The code of 1648 refers explicitly to the Bible which, according to the Puritans, also included aspects that could be applied to the legal systems of later periods.

In accordance with that biblical model, certain crimes were punishable by death. These included idolatry, witchcraft, blasphemy, bestiality, sodomy, adultery, rape, theft, treachery, bearing false witness with someone's death in mind, cursing or striking one's father or mother, stubbornness or rebelliousness on the part of a son towards his parents and murder, including killing by trickery or poisoning. The words of the Pentateuch were sometimes quoted literally (as, for example, in Deut. 21:18–21; 18:11; Lev. 20:13, 15; 16:27; Exod. 21:15–17); at other times, they are clearly discernible as forming the basis of the legislation (as, for example, in Deut. 15:12–14; 23:15–16; 25:2–3; Exod. 22:16; 21:26–27).[15]

This legislation led the Holy Commonwealth of Massachusetts to become known as a *theocracy*. John Cotton had formulated a draft legislation with the title of a *Model of Moses and his Judicials* as early as 1636. According to this *Model*, the only members of the Commonwealth who had an active and passive right to vote were the visible subjects of the Lord Jesus Christ, that is, those who could be recognised by their life-style and their confession of faith. These visible subjects also had to have committed themselves collectively to a personal covenant in their churches. According to Cotton Mather (1648–1728), the minister of the Second Church of Boston and the author of the *Magnalia Christi Americana* (1702), John Cotton had attempted to establish a theocracy that was as close as possible to that which was the glory of Israel, the special and chosen people.

Cotton's code of law was rejected, but *his theocratic philosophy* of the State to a very great extent determined the policy of the leading oligarchy—that, at least, was the opinion of Vernon L. Parrington, an author writing more than half a century ago.[16] Massachusetts did not, it is true, become a Hebrew State in which the political rights of the citizens were subjected to the demands made by religion and in which the preachers functioned in the last resort as a court in which the law of God was interpreted for the citizens as the subjects of Jehovah. The Puritan ministers have, however, been accused by historians of *religious intolerance* and of being tyrannical theocrats who were hostile towards the liberal natural law and democracy because they recognised only the sole rule of God's grace over human nature, which was, in their opinion, absolutely sinful. And these accusations are not entirely without foundation. The so-called antinomian crisis, which flared up around the figure of Anne Hutchinson and the banishment of Roger Williams illustrate very vividly the intolerance of the early years of the Massachusetts Colony.[17]

4. CONCLUSION

Leaving the corruption of the world and the Church activates in people a new consciousness of holiness which bears within itself the seeds of division. Intolerance with regard to evil makes holy men and their leaders hard and makes them exert discipline over others, even those in their own camp. The originally liberating inspiration is changed into a holy conformism and men are, if the need arises, forced to conform. Circumstances in the world are always calling on people to adapt and the demand for absolute holiness is always bringing them together and driving them apart. All that Williams wanted to do, after all, was to practise his religion with his own wife! The adaptations that the American Puritans had to make in the free world did not, however, in any way definitively eliminate the fundamentalist interpretation of the Bible! Exodus has, in the course of Christian history, proved to be not only a paradigm that gives hope, but also one that is very dangerous.[18]

Translated by David Smith

Notes

1. H. Stocks 'Exodusgemeinden' *RGG* II 832; K. Algermissen 'Exodusgemeinden' *LThK* III 131; H. Schröer 'Exodusmotiv' *TRE* 746–747.
2. M. W. Busch *Wunderliche Heilige. Religiöse und politische Geheimbünde und Secten* (Leipzig 1879) p. 122.
3. David A. Gerber 'The Pathos of Exile: Old Lutheran Refugees in the United States and South Australia' *Comparative Studies in Society and History* 26 (1984) 498–522.
4. *Ibid.* p. 509.
5. *Ibid.* p. 522.
6. Edmund S. Morgan *Puritan Dilemma: John Winthrop* (Boston 1958).
7. See the survey of books and articles in Ursula Brumm *Puritanismus und Literatur in Amerika* (Darmstadt 1973); Sacvan Bercovitch *The Puritan Origins of the American Self* (New Haven 1975).
8. L. D. Geller and P. J. Gomes *The Books of the Pilgrims* (New York 1975).
9. The work cited in note 8, at pp. 4–5; *Typology and Early American Literature* ed. Sacvan Bercovitch (Massachusetts 1972).
10. *The American Puritans. Their Prose and Poetry* ed. Perry Miller (New York 1956) pp. 1–19.
11. *Ibid.* pp. 36–47.
12. *Ibid.* pp. 28–35.
13. *Ibid.* pp. 78–83, 143–144.
14. *Ibid.* pp. 84–93.
15. George Lee Haskins *Law and Authority in Early Massachusetts* (New York 1960); partly reprinted in *Puritanism in Seventeenth-Century Massachusetts* ed. David D. Hall (New York 1968) pp. 61–70.
16. Vernon L. Parrington *Main Currents in American Thought* (New York 1927; 2nd. ed. 1955); partly reprinted in the work cited in note 15, edited by David D. Hall pp. 49–54; Perry Miller ed. *op. cit.* pp. 84–88, 59–77.
17. The work cited in note 10, edited by Perry Miller pp. 48–58; Edmund S. Morgan *Roger Williams. The Church and the State* (New York 1967); Norman Pettitt *The Heart Prepared: Grace and Conversion in Puritan Spiritual Life* (New Haven 1966).
18. J. Moltmann *Theology of Hope* (London 1969), Chap. V on Exodus communities; Y. Congar *Un Peuple messianique* (Paris 1975).

Wesley Kort

Exodus and its Biblical Paradigm

EXODUS, BY the American writer Leon Uris, holds a *three-fold relation to the Exodus narrative of the Bible*. First, it contains many references and allusions to biblical narratives and to Exodus in particular. In addition, the novel holds a structural similarity to its biblical counterpart. That is, the elements of both narratives have mythic qualities. Finally, *Exodus*, like its biblical paradigm, reveals motifs typical of creation myths.

The mythic characteristics of this novel of 1958 put it within the general interests of much twentieth-century fiction.[1] Indeed, even to say that the novel has scriptural pretensions would not exile it from what, as the critic Frank Kermode has recently made clear, are the intentions of some Modernist texts;[2] one thinks of the *Ulysses* of Joyce, of D. H. Lawrence's *The Rainbow*, and Mann's *Dr Faustus*.

In terms of its general mythical and scriptural characteristics, then, there is nothing very unusual about the novel. Yet, the material of the novel and the ways in which these qualities are produced and employed set it apart and deserve comment. The novel deals with events and actions leading to the emergence of Israel as a State in May 1948, and they possess an inherent interest of a highly emotional kind for many people. To combine fiction with such important and controversial material would be provocative enough, but to make myth of it is a matter of no small interest.

1. REFERENCES TO EXODUS

At the first and most obvious level, the novel contains many references to biblical narratives in general and to Exodus in particular. The event which initiates the novel's action in November 1946, is based on an historical actuality.[3] One of the ships used to carry Jewish emigrants to Palestine was an American excursion boat called *President Warfield* (after the company's president) and renamed the *Exodus 1947*. This boat provides an arresting conjunction between historical and biblical material. It initiates not only the novel's action but the rapid development of biblical counterparts throughout the novel as a whole. The reader is not surprised when the leader of the Jewish emigrants shouts to the British who retain the ship, 'LET MY PEOPLE GO' (p. 185).[4] Another character, Karen Hansen, notices that 'a fog bank enshrouded them as though God himself were giving cover ...' (p. 91). And the novel concludes with the celebration of Passover. In addition to such explicit references to Exodus, the novel's principal action, the migration of Jews to Palestine and the eventual founding of the State, has a shape analogous to Exodus. The British retain and impede the Jews, thereby becoming Pharaoh-like, and the need of the people to go to a place where they can receive a name, live with integrity, and be formed as a nation can be readily associated with the biblical narrative.

Aspects of this two-storeyed structure are provocative. First, it differs from the use of traditional or mythic materials in the novels by writers mentioned earlier. For example, when we encounter analogues to the biblical Exodus narrative in Faulkner's *Go Down Moses* or D. H. Lawrence's *Aaron's Rod*, these analogues enlarge and enrich the meaning and form of a particular by relating it to a traditional, even universal paradigm. Erich Kahler calls this an 'ascending symbolism'.[5] That is, the extension toward the mythic is generated from below. The particular has the power to generate a relation to the traditional or universal. While this can also be said of *Exodus*, we have more in this novel of what could be called a *symbolism from above*. That is, the novel evokes the biblical in order to grant meaning to the particular events and actions; the second story, the biblical analogues, grants to the novel's actions and events a certain legitimacy and authority. This use of the Bible sets the novel apart from the mainstream of modernist writing, however much it shares with that writing an interest in traditional materials and mythic characteristics.

2. STRUCTURAL SIMILARITIES

A less obvious but more important relation to the biblical Exodus is established through similarities in the novel's structural elements with their counterparts in the biblical story. These similarities grant mythic qualities to the novel's atmosphere, characters, tone and plot.[6]

Among the many things which could be said about the atmosphere of

Exodus, about what is possible or to be expected in the world it provides, is that it places the narrative on an ontological level somewhat above that of the reader. The Russian theorist, Mikhail Bakhtin, cites this as one of the distinguishing marks of epic or mythic narrative; the *ontology of the narrative* differs from that of the reader, is superior because marvellous things can happen in it which are not to be encountered in the reader's world.[7] Such an atmosphere is typical of biblical narrative, of course, and it is strongly present in Exodus. The reader stands below that in an ontologically less interesting world.

The ontology of *Exodus* is also above that of the reader. What one encounters here excedes normal expectations. One of the young Jewish militants in the novel, Ari Ben Canaan, tells his more sceptical colleague, David Ben Ami, that the course of Jewish history and destiny is itself a miracle (p. 26). The narrator tells us that the leadership of the British Zionist, Major P. P. Malcolm, was 'as though he were divinely guided as well as divinely inspired' (p. 300). Brigadier Bruce Sutherland, the half-Jewish, British observer and sympathiser, tells the American Kitty Fremont that 'when you see what they have done with this land you are not a realist if you do not believe in miracles' (p. 465). This is not simple hyperbole. The migration of Jews to Palestine, the settlement and the cultivation of the land, and the origination of the State are depicted as events beyond the range of normal expectations. Consequently, the specific references to divine favour and miracles articulate specifically the level which the whole of the narrative assumes for itself.

A similar point can be made concerning the *characters*. Many of them stand above the ordinary. Sutherland says of the Jewish leaders in the struggle: 'What a wonderful feeling of peace they must have. Something that we ordinary mortals can never know' (p. 194). And Kitty, when she observes these leaders, realises, by 'an electrifying revelation', that 'this was no army of mortals. These were the faces of Dan and Reuben and Judah and Ephraim! These were Samsons and Deborahs and Joabs and Sauls. It was the army of Israel, and no force on earth could stop them for the power of God was within them!' (p. 371). Again, this is not simple hyperbole. A direct tie is made between them, therefore, and biblical characters such as Moses or Gideon who had divine mandates and carried into their conflicts a power far more than their own.

The *tone*, along with the novel's atmosphere and characters, contributes to this elevation above the ordinary. We can see this particularly in the *point of view*. An omniscient point of view, as critics and theorists such as J. Hillis Miller and Jacques Derrida have made clear, grants to the narrator a divine perspective.[8] Such a narrator knows and controls all. The perspective is not relative, conditioned or subject to correction by the perspectives of others. Omniscient point of view is crucial to biblical narratives and serves greatly to grant them authority. The point of view includes God, and it must, to do that, itself be divinely attributable. Omniscient point of view grants authority to a narrative by concealing the conditioned perspective which any narrative or text has.

Point of view has a similar effect on *Exodus*. It enables the narrator to stand above the individual stories within the novel and direct them toward the one, inclusive goal. There are many embedded stories in the novel: the personal histories of several characters, the migration of Jews to Palestine in the closing decades of the nineteenth and the opening decades of the twentieth centuries, the history of British involvement in the Middle East, and the development of the Zionist movement. This technique allows the narrator to stand above a vast temporal and spatial expanse and to orchestrate the individual actions and events toward the central concern of his narrative. All events lead to, even conspire to bring about, the settlement of the land and the origins of Statehood. Furthermore, the narrator is able to narrate not only the thoughts of characters but unrelated events which are made simultaneous by the unity which his distant but sure-handed control provides.

Finally, the *plot* of the novel is also heightened. This is done by allowing a particular series of events to be decisive and of universal significance. This is also true of the Exodus narrative in the Bible. Certainly, the plot gives us the move of people from their position of servitude in Egypt to their new freedom and life together in the wilderness. But a more general paradigm can also be discerned. The plot renders an exchange in the *making and overcoming of distinctions or separations*. By the end of the narrative one kind of separation and lack of separation has been exchanged for another. In Egypt the word of Yahweh and the course of the people's lives are separated. This separation of event from intention is overcome in the narrative, particularly through the way in which the action of each episode is first described by Yahweh to Moses and then occurs. In the Exodus word and event, divine intention and human experience, are united. Conversely, there is also a lack of separation in Egypt, namely, between the Hebrews and their Egyptian neighbours. In the narrative, through such means as the sign of blood, the two are separated from one another—'that you may learn that the Lord makes a distinction between Egypt and Israel' (11:7). That is, above the particular pattern of the plot, the delivery of the people from Egypt, is this more general pattern, and the more general pattern allows for the participation in the story of later generations. While the people need not be delivered from Egypt annually, they do have to experience annually reversals or exchanges within this complex of separations and identities.

The *Exodus* of Uris also combines a particular and a general pattern in the plot. Both can be related to the Exodus narrative in the Bible. The particular is the wresting of the people from the retention of the Pharaoh-like British and their move from conditions of hardship and victimisation toward becoming a newly formed people. But the more general pattern can also be detected.

The history of the Jews from biblical times until the present is indicated in the novel as a time free from intention and design. Events and meaning are separated. *Meaningful time* begins again with the settlement of Palestine by Jews. In addition, during this in-between time a lack of clear distinction developed between non-Jews and Jews. What it means to be a Jew was derived from non-Jews, whether positively or negatively. So, Karen Hansen's father typifies Jews who accommodated themselves to a non-Jewish world and lived in the illusion that it would protect and respect them. Dov Landau's father had the meaning of Jewishness thrust upon him by ghetto life. Either way, the position and meaning of the Jew is derived from non-Jews. This situation is exchanged for a form of life and identity in Palestine by which the meaning of 'Jew' is not derived from non-Jews. Again, while the British need not periodically be overcome, it may periodically be necessary for Jewish readers to experience an exchange of actions and events which lack meaningful intentions for those which have a clear purpose, and an exchange of lack of distinction from or domination by non-Jews for the freedom to be a Jew or a Jewish people independently.

3. WHAT EFFECTS DO THESE QUALITIES PRODUCE?

Now that we have seen how the novel presents at all four of its structural elements—atmosphere, character, tone, and plot—mythic qualities or effects and shares such qualities with the biblical story, we can go on to ask a more general question. What effects do these qualities produce? The most direct answer to the question is that we have here a narrative that resembles a *creation myth*. In this respect as well *Exodus* can be compared to the biblical Exodus story, since it also employs creation motifs in its depictions of God's redemption of his people.

First of all, the biblical narrative depicts a struggle between the God who forms a people and those powers which oppose his creative work. Both opposing powers have influence over the conditions of life. The struggle is replete with cosmological associations, especially, of course, through the plagues. The contending powers have jurisdiction not only over people but also over cosmic matters. And the song of Moses suggests a relation between Yahweh's adversary and thoose chaotic waters which, in the opening verses of

Genesis 1, had to be pushed back. The Exodus narrative also suggests origination in the many allusions to birth: the doorways marked with blood, the first born, and passage through the waters. Finally, the temporal setting, the spring of the year, the beginning of the new year for ancient Israel, ties together the redemption from Egypt and cosmogony by means of a New Year celebration.[9]

Exodus shares many of these creation motifs. The origination of a newly unified people and of a new nation is opposed by the British and the Arabs. The principal action of the novel is the conflict with these adversaries. In addition, new life and identity are created in and for Jews by these events. At the close of the second world war European Jews were, according to Sutherland, a 'beaten people—at the end of the line—dazed, withered, exhausted' (p. 24). They are 'motherless, fatherless, loveless' (p. 590). 'To them, all Europe has become a coffin' (p. 82). In addition, the land itself is in need of recreation. On arrival in Palestine the Jews find it wasted, 'a land of festering stagnated swamps and eroded hills and rock-filled fields and unfertile earth caused by a thousand years of Arab and Turkish neglect' (p. 225–6). The Arabs contributed nothing to the land, 'building on other people's civilisations' (p. 329). The land is redeemed and recreated.

While both the British and the Arabs are the antagonists in this creation scenario, the Arabs can more directly be related than the British to the chaos or evil which must be pushed back if the new order is to be formed. They are depicted as unruly, undisciplined, dirty, and unproductive. 'Their courage was mob frenzy' (p. 574). Opposed to them, Karen tells Kitty, is the work of God to establish in this new nation 'a bridge between darkness and light' (p. 615). The purpose of the new people is to establish 'on the frontiers' a society which will 'guard His laws which are the cornerstone of man's moral existence' (p. 615). Thus, the conflict with the British but especially with the Arabs is cast in the form of a *cosmic struggle* between the forces of light and divine order, on the one hand, and the forces of darkness and moral chaos, on the other.

4. THE VALUES OF KITTY FREMONT

More should be said, however, about the creation motifs in *Exodus*. Here the otherwise *enigmatic centrality of the American Kitty Fremont* becomes clear. This Protestant from Indiana, the 'all-American girl' from 'the all-American Midwest', has a significant role to play in the novel. At the most obvious level her presence implicates Christian interests in the Israeli cause. Kitty is conscious of the associations of many places, especially in the Galilee, with the life and ministry of Jesus. In addition, her movement from a neutrality towards the Jewish goals of settlement and nationhood to a position of sympathy and support represents a significant apologetic strategy, for she is convinced as a neutral observer by what the reader is lead to think of as the merits of the case.[10] It can also be said that as a Protestant, a Christian, that is, for whom the history of Christianity from biblical times to the present has less authority than that history would have for a Catholic Christian, Kitty is able tacitly to reinforce the critical move Uris makes of undercutting the significance of the long period from biblical time to the present in which the Jewish presence in and claim to the land weakened.

Kitty also contributes to the *sense of animosity* in the novel. It should be noticed that the most grievously negative comments concerning Arabs are made by Kitty. She observes, at one point, 'how pathetic the dirty little Arab children were beside the robust youngsters of Gan Dafna' (p. 361). The Bedouins strike her as 'the dregs of humanity. The women were encased in black robes—and layers of dirt. She was not able to smell the goats but she was able to smell the women' (p. 366). She contrasts the cleanliness of Jewish settlements to 'the filth and decay of most Arab villages' (p. 453). Such comments are all the more striking, due to the fact that Kitty is otherwise presented as a compassionate and objective person.

Comments such as these are, quite expectedly, offensive to Arab readers.[11] One consequence of attributing them to Kitty is that her identity dissociates prejudice from Jewish sources. But more may be involved in the strongly anti-Arab comments of this American character. Kitty appears to impose on the Israeli-Arab conflicts the model of the settlement of America. The Europeans are to the American Indians as the European Jews are to the Arabs. If so, the role of the Exodus narrative in the novel yields to the myth of pushing back the barbarians on American soil and creating a civilised society worthy of the land it appropriates. The Exodus, thereby, is given a *particularly American ideological shape*.

The *background of American paradigms* in the novel comes more clearly into view when we inquire concerning the nature of the new society which the Jewish emigrants are establishing in Palestine. It has three predominant characteristics. One of them is responsibility, even reverence, for the *natural environment*. Much attention is given in the novel to the strong feeling for the land and its nurture which the Jews who migrate and settle there share. This attachment is neither only textual or historical. The people arriving there are not accustomed to close association with nature. Commitment to the land ties the society closely to its natural environment.

The second characteristic of this new society is its *cultural complexity*. It is 'the merging point of a hundred civilisations ...' (p. 346). 'The old and the new jammed together' (p. 348). People from 'seventy-four nations' (p. 596) constitute this society. It is even suggested that fleeing Palestinian Arabs, had they not been led astray by their self-seeking leaders, would have found a place in the new order (p. 574). And Christians, as Kitty makes clear, are included as well.

Finally, the society is oriented by a vision of a *new human future*. The people work selflessly for the sake of later generations who will realise a dignity, freedom, and sense of corporate responsibility unattained in the past. 'From the moment the downtrodden set foot on the soil of Israel they were granted a human dignity and freedom that most of them had never known, and this equality fired them with a drive and purpose without parallel in man's history' (p. 596). It is for this future society and not for personal gain that people labour. They have as their goal only 'Israel and tomorrow' (p. 608).

Any student of American history and culture will recognise these three affirmations as *central to the image of America*, especially in the nineteenth century, as a land of promise. The land as a potential garden, the cultural richness created by interactions between differing kinds of people, and orientation to the future, to the ideal for individual and society, form the agenda of the American spiritual enterprise.[12] This myth of America, the novel implies, has shifted location. Kitty, who throughout the novel intends to return to America, decides toward the end to stay in Israel. She need not return, for what America once promised Israel now provides.

The *Exodus* of Leon Uris, then, is related to its biblical paradigm in three ways. First, parallels are drawn between the novel's situations, events, characters and actions, and biblical counterparts. Less obvious but more important to the power and meaning of the narrative, all of its elements, in ways similar to the biblical Exodus, are granted mythic qualities. Most important, however, is the transposition of the Exodus paradigm into a new key. The creation of Israel provides, for Uris, the hope for human life which America once promised.

Notes

1. Of the many books which deal with this matter, see especially Eric Gould *Mythical Intentions in Modern Literature* (Princeton 1981).

2. Frank Kermode *The Genesis of Secrecy: On the Interpretation of Narrative* (Cambridge, Mass. 1979).

3. See Ruth Gruber *Destination Palestine: The Story of the Haganah Ship Exodus 1947* (New York 1948).

4. Leon Uris *Exodus* (Garden City, New York 1958). Quotations in the essay will be parenthetically noted and refer to this edition of the novel.

5. Erich Kahler *The Inward Turn of Narrative* (Princeton 1973).

6. The understanding of narrative as a system of discourse constituted by these

four elements is detailed in my *Narrative Elements and Religious Meaning* (Philadelphia 1975).

7. Mikhail Bakhtin *The Dialogic Imagination: Four Essays*. Translated by Caryl Emerson and Michael Holquist (Austin 1981).

8. See Jacques Derrida 'Of an Apocalyptic Tone Recently Adopted in Philosophy' in *Derrida and Biblical Studies* ed. Robert Detweiler Semeia 23 (Society of Biblical Literature 1982), pp. 63–97, and J. Hillis Miller *The Form of Victorian Fiction* (Notre Dame and London 1968).

9. The clearest and most succinct analysis of traditional narratives as creation myths can be found in the work of the historian of religion Mircea Eliade. See especially his *Myth and Reality* (New York 1963) and his *Le Mythe de l'éternal retour: archétypes et répétition* (Paris 1949).

10. I am indebted to my colleague, Professor Kalman Bland, for pointing out that this use of non-Jewish approbation for Jewish interests and beliefs is a common, traditional strategy in Jewish apologetic literature.

11. See Aziz S. Sahwell *Exodus: A Distortion of Truth* (New York 1960).

12. For a study of the importance of these three beliefs for American literature and religious thought see my *Moral Fiber: Character and Belief in Recent American Fiction* (Philadelphia 1982).

PART III

Contemporary Movements

Enrique Dussel

Exodus as a Paradigm in Liberation Theology

THE RE-READING of Exodus runs through the history of the Latin American church. In the middle of the sixteenth century, shortly after the conquest, the holy bishop of Popayan, Juan del Valle, said that the primitive inhabitants of the region were 'treated worse than the slaves in Egypt'.[1] The valiant revolutionary, the Inca Tupac Amaru, in the decree by which he summoned hundreds of thousands of indigenous people to rise against Spain in Peru on 14 November 1780, wrote:

> The Catholic zeal of a son of the Church, as a professed Christian in most holy baptism ... hoping that many others will shake off the yoke of this Pharaoh, the magistrates, I have set forth to speak for and defend the whole kingdom ... The purposes of my sound intention are [to win] for my nation complete freedom from all forms of oppression.[2]

When we reach our own century we find the expression 'land flowing with milk and honey' at the end of the Sandinista anthem in Nicaragua. Or we have Fidel Castro's reference, in his defence, *History Will Forgive Me*, to

> the 100,000 small farmers who live [in 1956] and die working a land that is not theirs, contemplating it sadly as Moses did the promised land ...[3]

That is why, as part of this tradition of the Latin American people, liberation theology from its very beginning understood the paradigm of the Exodus as its fundamental schema. So strong is this sense that it is even criticised for this continual return to a re-reading of Exodus.

83

1. THE RELEVANCE OF THE EXODUS PARADIGM FOR THE THIRD WORLD TODAY

The Exodus appears as a central point in *African liberation theology*,[4] and we should not forget that the setting for the Exodus story was actual North Africa. The same can be said of *Asian liberation theology*,[5] where, perhaps even to a greater extent than in Latin America, the oppression of the poor is a blatant fact, beyond concealing. In *Latin America*, from the beginning, we have always come back to Exodus. I recall that as early as 1967 I used to begin my courses at IPLA (CELAM's Instituto Pastoral Latinoamericano in Quito) with exegesis of Exodus;[6] there one could find, spelt out, the main categories of liberation theology. In the same way, at different times, liberation theologians have always had to refer to the basic texts of Exodus.[7]

According to Rubem Alves in 1970,

The Exodus was the experience which created the consciousness of the people of Israel. The people formed in the structuring centre which determined its way of organising time and space. Note that I am not saying simply that the Exodus is part of the contents of the consciousness of the people of Israel. If that were the case, the Exodus would be one item of information among others. More than an item of information, it is *its structuring centre*, in that it determines the integrating logic, the principle of organisation and interpretation of historical experience. That is why the Exodus does not persist as a secondary experience ... It has come to be *the paradigm* for the interpretation of *all space and all time*.[8]

Sixteen years ago the great Brazilian Protestant theologian pointed explicitly (even in his use of the term 'paradigm') to the topic which concerns us. We shall examine it in stages.

By 'paradigm' we mean the generative matrix or 'schema' (in something like the Kantian sense), the *structure* which, from fundamental *categories*, originates a fixed number of *relations* which become generative, not only of a theology, but also of the everyday hermeneutic of the Christian people's faith.

There are essentially six of these categories: (1) Egypt and the Pharaonic class (Ph), the dominators, the sinners (Exod. 1:8); (2) the slaves (S), the exploited, the just (Exod. 1:11); (3) the prophet, Moses (M) (Exod 2:1ff.); (4) God (G), who listens and converts (Exod. 3:1ff.); (5) the passage (P) through the desert, the passover, the trials, the ambiguity—such a contemporary theme—of the priest Aaron (Exod. 12:37ff.); (6) the promised land (L) (Exod. 3:8).

Simplified diagram of the Exodus 'paradigm'

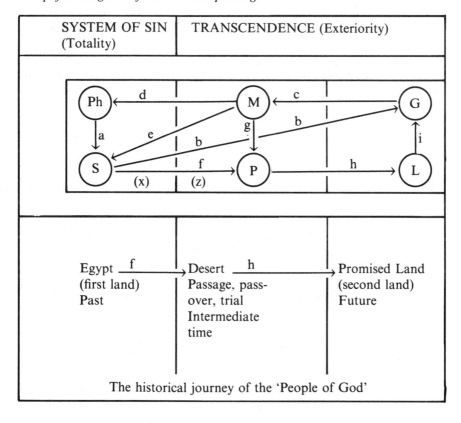

There are eight *relations* which, arising from the *categories*, make up the *structure* of the paradigm: (a) domination or sin (Exod. 1:1–22); (b) the cry of the people (Exod. 3:7); (c) conversion, the call of the word to the prophet (Exod. 2:11–4:17); (d) challenge to the dominator, the sinner (Exod. 4:18–6:1); (e) challenge to the people of God (Exod. 6:2–27); (f) departure, liberation (Exod. 7:8ff.); (g) critical prophetic action, even against the priest Aaron (prophet-priest dialectic, continuing throughout the passage through the desert); (h) entry, the building of the new system (Josh. 3:16ff.); (i) salvation, the kingdom, the community of life, which may be another Egypt (1 Sam. 8:10–18) and so splits: the historical promised land (always liable to be surpassed) and the kingdom of God (the absolute, only fully realised after history).

However, as Alves indicates, there are three space-time areas which organise the discourse, praxis: (1) Egypt as the past, the 'first land', (2) the desert as the 'intermediate time' and space of passage; (3) the promised land as the utopian term, the future, the 'second land'.

The totality of the discourse, of historical praxis, of the paradigm, has a *subject*, 'the children of Israel',[9] the people of the oppressed liberating themselves from the slavery of exploitation, of sin, in an alliance with their God:

> I will go down with you to Egypt, and I will also bring you up again (Gen. 46:4).

The paradigm can be seen, theologically, in the re-reading which the Bible performs of itself:

> By faith Moses, when he was grown up, refused to be called the son of Pharaoh's daughter, choosing rather to share ill-treatment with the people of God than to enjoy the fleeting pleasures of sin ... By faith he left Egypt ... By faith he kept the Passover and sprinkled the blood ... By faith the people crossed the Red Sea as if on dry land ... By faith the walls of Jericho fell down (Heb. 11:24–30).

For us Latin Americans, certainly, the text of Exodus makes a powerful call on our attention. The reason is clear:

> The liberation of Israel is a political action. It is the breaking away from a situation of despoliation and misery and the beginning of the construction of a just and fraternal society. It is the suppression of disorder and the creation of a new order. The initial chapters of Exodus describe the oppression in which the Jewish people lived in Egypt, in that 'land of slavery' (13:3; 20:2; Deut. 5:6): repression (1:10–11), alienated work (5:6–14), humiliations (1:13–14), enforced birth control policy (1:15–22). Yahweh then awakens the vocation of a liberator: Moses.[10]

Let us now see how, historically and in practice, liberation theology has moved in and across the Exodus paradigm.

2. DIACHRONIC UNFOLDING OF THE PARADIGM

It should not be thought that everything was present from the beginning, or that everything has already taken place. There has been a *history* (a 'diachrony' of the 'synchronous' moments of the paradigm) which still has to be written. What follows are introductory notes for that history.

In my view, the liberation theologians, as a 'school of prophets'—not as individuals of genius, since they are a community phenomenon in Latin America—have *gradually been 'taking consciousness' of the categories and relations indicated.* They have been semantically deepening their content and, as a result, starting from the 'consciousness of the Christian people' of Latin America themselves, the theology has been growing alongside, starting from and following the historical praxis of that people. Everything could not be expressed in the sixties because the Christian people had not lived through fundamental historical spiritual experiences. History determined the explicit gaining of consciousness of the moments of the Exodus paradigm in liberation theology. No theologians from one Latin American country alone could perform this task; it was the communal achievement of the 'school of prophets' stimulating each other, and based on the experience of the Christian people of various countries. Underplaying some theologians in liberation theology, or exaggerating the importance of some countries, impoverishes an ecclesial and continental phenomenon which is already a 'historical fact' which in a short time has gone round the small world of theology, and indeed of the Church.

On at least five levels there has been a *diachronic maturation* in the gaining of theological consciousness of the structures of the paradigm. First, there has been a move from 'personal' (abstract individual) and 'subjective' experience of *poverty (as a virtue) to poverty as a requirement for the whole Church.* The 'Church of the poor', it is now seen, must be a poor church (the pope, the Vatican, bishops, priests, activists, with a spirit of poverty, without any triumphalism, giving away unnecessary wealth, land, etc.). Secondly, there has been a move from this 'subjective' poverty, as a virtue or 'spiritual infancy', to the objective fact of 'the poor', *other people.* It is no longer Moses poor in the desert, but Moses discovering the poor man being ill-treated by the official (Exod. 2:11–12). Thirdly, there has been a move from the poor discovered in the spiritual experience of the Gospel to the definition of these poor (thanks to the hermeneutical mediation of the social sciences) as a *'class'*—first in specific countries—and subsequently as a *'people'* in other Latin American countries. The move has been from 'subjectivity' (poverty-virtue) to 'objectivity' (poor-class-people).

Fourthly, there has been a movement from these poor, the class, the people, as object of an 'option-for' (I, subject, opt-for another), to the affirmation of these poor, this class, this people, as the *'subject' of the Church and history* (a move from the people as 'object' to the people as 'subject'). Only at this point do we have the emergence of the 'Church of the poor', not the 'poor' Church of the Vatican II period with the emphasis on the poverty of bishops, priests, etc., but the Church which has as its 'privileged subject' the historical Christian people, made up of the real poor, flesh, bone, blood and oppression, whom the hierarchical structures (pope, Vatican, bishops) have to serve and keep as a point of reference. (A necessary stage here was the 'popular Church', though this has now been superseded.)

And, finally, the fifth aspect is that the diachrony is perhaps more in accord with Exodus. In other words, the Christian people are re-reading scripture in terms of their *actual historical situation*. Oppression, dictatorships, exploitation without hope, form a *Latin American Egypt* (S): today in Chile, but in 1976 in Brazil, Argentina, Nicaragua, etc. Pre-revolutionary situations are the Egyptian 'plagues' (today Guatemala, for example—point x on arrow f, the beginning of liberation). Revolutionary situations in the strict sense as in El Salvador are the going out into the desert (point z on arrow f). The wandering in the desert, the violent persecution by Pharaoh's armies, could be compared with the 'contras' in Nicaragua (this was the interpretation of the basic ecclesial communities in Esteli), Aaron's treason (then the priest, now the bishop?), the prophet's rage (Miguel D'Escoto?), etc. Finally there is the building of a new order (before the First Cuban National Ecclesial Encounter, ENEC, in February 1986 we seemed to catch sight already of a new order, which, however, is never the final kingdom). We shall look at these elements in turn in summary form, more as suggestions than a finished analysis.

3. THE FIRST SEMANTIC SHIFT: FROM THE 'INDIVIDUAL' TO THE 'POOR' CHURCH

In what was still the prehistory of liberation theology, in the 1950s, many people went through the spiritual experience of a *radical demand for poverty*. Examples are Charles de Foucauld, a Franciscan renewal in various areas of the Church, the presence of French worker priests in the refugee camps during the second world war. I myself was with Paul Gauthier in Nazareth between 1959 and 1961.[11] Our rule of life there was the text: 'The Spirit of the Lord has anointed me to evangelise the poor' (See Isa. 61:1; Luke 4:18). Working in the Arab *Sikkun* of Nazareth (as a carpenter) or as fishermen on Tiberias (in the Ginnosar Kibbutz), we discovered the poor Jesus and Jesus the poor worker. At the beginning of the Second Vatican Council Mgr Hakim, the bishop of Nazareth, Mgr Hammer of Tournai and others, including Helder Camara, launched through the Nazareth team the idea of the 'Church of the poor', which Pope John XXIII took up personally. It was a personal, individual requirement of poverty, accepted by people from the pope and cardinals down to bishops, priests, religious and lay activists. The archbishop of Medellin left his episcopal palace and went to live in a poor district. Mgr Manuel Larrain distributed his diocese's land for the sake of poverty, bishops began to sell their gold pectoral crosses and replaced them with crosses without precious metal. It was a shift from personal poverty, from the 'spiritual childhood' of Teresa of Lisieux, which made such a great impact on us in our adolescence, to community and ecclesial poverty on the part of the universal institution. The goal was a non-triumphalist Church, humble, a servant, poor. This took place in many parts of Latin America from 1952 to 1965, and it later had repercussions in the first works of liberation theology.

4. SECOND SHIFT: FROM 'POVERTY' TO 'THE POOR'

'Subjective' poverty (on the part of the Christian or of the church) was still something of a preparatory stage (M in the schema or paradigm). It was the 'Put off your shoes from your feet' (Exod. 3:5), a demand and conversion, an anticipatory spiritual experience, and as such the origin of the liberation theology which was to come. But now the prophet (M) in the desert, converted, can begin a discourse. At the beginning the theme was 'faith and politics', the possibility of political commitment, on the part of university students (YCS) and worker activists (YCW). The Cuban revolution (in 1959, the same time as John XXIII launched the idea of a council) had encouraged many young people to go beyond a subjectivist spirituality; it was the time for action—remember Camilo Torres: faith and charity combined with effectiveness. The 'objectivity' of the demand for commitment led to the use of the social sciences, of even Marxist analysis if necessary (remember the Brazilian Acao Popular of the early sixties).

I believe that it was only when a revolutionary political idea was able to combine synthetically with the spiritual experience of subjective poverty that something fundamental took place. The idea was 'the poor'.[12] I recall Assmann's very sensible criticism of the ambiguity of the category 'poor'. By that time it had not been assimilated by liberation theology outside Argentina. The El Escorial meeting (1972) broached the idea explicitly: it was the first time that so many liberation theologians had come together. There the *idea of 'the poor' exploded as a category and a reality*.

It was now possible to talk, not of a 'poor' Church (a subjective and hierarchical approach), but of an 'option *for the poor*' (an objective approach). Note, however, that if the Church, the prophet (M), opts for the slave (S and arrow e on the diagram), that means that it is not yet poor by birth. It is a moment of maturation, but in no sense the end of the process or of the objective conversion of the Church.

5. THIRD SHIFT: FROM 'THE POOR' TO 'CLASS' AND 'PEOPLE'

Who are 'the poor'? The abstract poor or real people? Very soon, following El Escorial, where the idea was raised, the answer was given: *the poor are also a social 'class'*. But they can also be '*the people*'. The term 'poor', even in Marxist thought, cannot be identified with a social 'class', but has been used ambiguously to take advantage of its social and Gospel relevance. A Chilean and Peruvian strand, at the height of the Popular Unity government, placed more stress on class analysis. The southern cone, Argentine, line (with the experience of the return of Peronism) tended towards the category 'people'. 'Classism' had a partial aspect, as did 'populism'. What is certain is that both currents merged in their best aspects, around 1973. 'I have heard the cry of my people' (see the Exodus expression), the document of the bishops of the Brazilian North-East, marks, approximately, the beginning of the spiritual experience of a 'popular Church'. The Argentine element combined with the 'class' line but, at the same time, the category 'poor', previously absent, now became central.

In reality there was a twofold maturation (of *S*). On the one hand, as we have noted, the 'poor' Church (subjective) opted for 'the poor' (objective), but 'the poor'—thanks to the mediation of the social sciences and the political commitments of Christians—were now seen as a 'class', and even more, 'the people'. The idea of 'the poor' had been filled out, made historical, identifiable. It was now real, Latin American: '*the Latin American Christian people*'.

In addition, the Church, from being subjectively poor, now discovered itself as 'the people of God', as the (objectively) popular Church. This is no longer an option (options are made by the prophet of the prophetic Church, *M*), but an affirmation of itself: the people has become the subject (the *S* of the diagram is now the subject, 'the children of Israel'). In other words, the poor, the class, the people, for whom the objective option is made, *now became subjects*. This is a subjectivisation of the process, but not now focused on virtue, the individual virtue of poverty, as in the 1950s, but the subjectivisation of the poor themselves, who now have the 'consciousness' of being the people of God, the most hidden part of the Church, the necessary reference for evangelisation. The poor, who were evangelised (the 'basic ecclesial communities', etc.) *now become the evangelisers*.[13]

This last step, after the Nicaraguan revolution (1979), brings a realisation that it is no longer necessary to speak of a popular Church, and there is a return to John XXIII's description 'the Church of the poor'. Now, however, 'of the poor' does not mean just that the Church is poor, but—and this is fundamental—that the real, historical poor are the privileged 'subject' of the

Church itself. The implication is that the slaves (*S*) are 'subjects' of a possible process of liberation (arrow *f*).

The 'praxis of liberation' then also started to change direction, from the liberating praxis of prophets and heroes to the praxis of the people themselves in their liberation. It would be easy to demonstrate this 'semantic shift' in all the liberation theologians. Liberation theology, as a humble expression of this praxis, can also fulfil a critical prophetic function which enables this praxis to be reproduced (arrow *g*).

Translated by Francis McDonagh

Notes

1. See E. Dussel *El episcopado latinoamericano y la liberación de los pobres* (CRT, Mexico 1979).
2. Quoted in B. Lewis *La rebelión de Tupac Amaru*, (SELA Buenos Aires 1967) pp. 452–53. See E. Dussel, 'Introducción general' *Historia General de la Iglesia en América Latina* (Sigueme, Salamanca 1983) pp. 268–80.
3. Fidel Castro *La revolución cubana 1953–62* (Era, Mexico 1976) p. 39.
4. See Jean-Marc Ela 'Une Lecture africaine de l'Exode' in *Le Cri de l'homme africain* (L'Harmattan, Paris 1980) pp. 40–51.
5. Tissa Balasuriya *Planetary Theology* (Orbis Books, New York 1984) p. 184; Cyris Hee Suk Moon *Minjung Theology* (Orbis Books, New York 1986) p. 120. Also Emerito Nacpitl 'A Gospel for the New Filipino' in *Asian Voices in Theology* (Orbis Books, New York 1976) p. 129.
6. See E. Dussel *History and Theology of Liberation* (Orbis Books, New York 1976) pp. 155ff.
7. See Hugo Assman *Teologia desde la praxis de la liberación* (Sígueme, Salamanca 1973) pp. 54–55: 'Opresión en Egito, Exodo'; Samuel Silva Gotay *El pensamiento cristiano revolucionario en America Latina* (Sígueme, Salamanca 1981) pp. 141–47: 'La liberación del éxodo centro estructurante de la fe'; H. Bojorge 'Exodo y liberación' *Vispera* 19–20 (1970) 33ff; Andres Lanson *Liberar a los oprimidos* (Kaitas, Buenos Aires 1967); Pedro Negre 'Biblia y liberación' in *Cristianismo y sociedad* 24–25 (1970) pp. 49ff; see the reference to the Exodus in the meeting on liberation theology (at the beginning on development) in November 1969 in Mexico: *Inf. Cath. Internat.* 351 (1970) pp. 12ff; Jorge Pixley *Exodo. Una lectura evangélica y popular* (CUPSA, Mexico 1983); 'El Nuevo Testamento y el socialismo' *El apostol* 3/1 (1973) 14ff; R. Sartor 'Exodo-liberación: tema de actualidad para una reflexión teológica' *Revista Biblica* 139/32 (1971) 73–77; Luís Rivera 'La liberación en el éxodo' *Revista Biblica* 139/32 (1971) pp. 13–26. The list could be endless, since reference to the Exodus in liberation theology is continual. Even the second Instruction of the Congregation for the Doctrine of the Faith ('Instruction on Christian Freedom and Liberation', 22 Mar 1986) deals with it in its para. 44: 'The exodus and Yahweh's liberating acts'. Nor can

we forget Porfirio Miranda *Marx and the Bible* (Orbis Books, New York 1974; SCM, London 1977 pp. 78–88ff; 'The God of the Exodus'); Elsa Tamez *La Biblia de los oprimidos* (DEI, San Jose 1979); Segundo Galilea 'La liberación como encuentro de la política y la contemplación' *Espiritualidad y Liberación* (DEI, San Jose 1982) pp. 45ff; Ignacio Ellacuria *Freedom Made Flesh* (Orbis Books, New York 1976) p. 16; for the position of Ernesto Cardenal, see Phillip Berryman *The Religious Roots of Rebellion* (Orbis Books, New York 1984) pp. 20, 23, etc.; S. Croato 'Liberacion y libertad. Reflexiones hermeneúticas en torno al Antiguo Testamento' *Revista Biblica* 32 (1971) 3–7; *Liberacion y libertad* (Mundo Nuevo, Buenos Aires 1973).

    8. In 'Pueblo de Dios y la liberación del homre' *Fichas ISAL* 3/26 (1979) p. 9.

    9. See J. Pixley *Exodo*, p. 19.

    10. Gustavo Gutierrez *A Theology of Liberation* (Orbis Books, New York 1973 and SCM Press, London 1974) pp. 155–56. See also the texts on pp. 155–60 and 287ff.

    11. See Methol Ferre 'La Iglesia latinoamericana de Rio a Puebla (1955–79)' *Historia de la Iglesia* ed. Fliche-Martin (EDICEP, Valencia 1981) suppl. vol. 1 pp. 697–725; Gustavo Gutierrez 'Teología de la Liberación y ciencias sociales', duplicated text. See Paul Gauthier *Les Pauvres, Jésus et l'Eglise* (Ed. Universitaires, Paris 1963) pp. 101ff: 'De Nazaret vers Rome'. I remember the little community of Paul, Andrés and myself—which I left in 1961 to start my theological studies in France. The community's rule of life contains the following statement at the beginning: 'Its aim is to live the Gospel in the light of that text from Luke 4 in which Jesus, quoting Isaiah 61, reveals his messianic anointing and his mission to evangelise *the poor*' (Gauthier p. 113).

    12. This was made possible by the convergence of the Nazareth experience (1959–61) and a reading of E. Levinas (1969): the 'poor' (Isa. 61:1; Luke 4:18), the Latin American poor, the poor as real people and as a theological category (see E. Dussel *Para una ética de la liberación latinoamericana* (1970) (Buenos Aires 1973) I, Chap. 3).

    13. See Jon Sobrino *Resurreción de la verdadera Iglesia. Los pobres, lugar teológico de la ecclesiología* (Santander 1981).

Josiah Young

Exodus as a Paradigm for the Black Theology

> One of these mornings, five o'clock,
> Dis ole world gonna reel and rock,
> Pharaoh's army got drownded,
> Oh Mary, don't you weep.

MY PURPOSE in this essay is twofold. First, after noting aspects of the story of the Exodus, I will discuss the specific, historic context that partly explains why Exodus is a paradigm for Black theologians' essential belief that God is liberator and unequivocally on the side of the oppressed. Second, I will propose that the epic theme of the Exodus has certain systematic implications for Black theologians. Throughout, I will focus on aspects of the theologies of James Cone and J. Deotis Roberts.

1. PHARAOH'S ARMY DROWNED IN THE RED SEA

The drowning of Pharaoh's army is part of a biblical witness to God's liberation of Jacob's descendents from Egyptian slavery and is the *central liberating event of Exodus*, of which the dominant character is Moses. God sends Moses to tell Pharaoh to release the enslaved Hebrews. Afflicting the Egyptians with plagues and hardening Pharaoh's heart, God by way of Moses directs a stupendous drama which intensifies with the death of the Egyptians' first born. Mourning the death of his first child, Pharaoh finally sets the Hebrews free. However, Pharaoh's heart is again hardened. Reneging on his decision, Pharaoh races in his chariots to re-enslave the Hebrews. With the sea in front of them and Pharaoh rapidly gaining on them from behind, the children of Jacob felt trapped. 'Moses said to the people, "Fear not, stand firm, and see the salvation of the Lord, which he will work for you today. ... The Lord will fight for you, and you have only to be still" ' (Exod. 14:13–14). God directed Moses to lift his staff of liberation over the waters. They parted. The children of Jacob, carrying Joseph's bones, crossed over en route to the Promised Land. Pharaoh's army drowned, and the Hebrew children knew their God was the almighty God of liberation.

The story of the God of Moses has been embraced by Blacks of the United States. The biblical account of God's mighty acts on behalf of the Hebrew children has captured their imagination. Afro-Americans' historic experience of gross exploitation within the Americas has resulted in their faithful focus on the Exodus; they have felt justified in their identification with the people of Moses. If, they have reasoned, God destroyed Pharaoh, will not our oppressor also be destroyed? Indeed, Exodus is the clearest Old Testament example of both God's sensitivity to the oppressed and destruction of the oppressor. Thus, Exodus has over the centuries been in Afro-America the *critical text revelatory of God's action in history on behalf of the oppressed.*

Black theologians have inherited the historic Black faith that God is a God of liberation. Faced with the question, 'How could a just God allow such heinous oppression of Black people?', Black theologians appeal to the Exodus, which vividly depicts God's destruction of the oppressor. Indeed, J. Deotis Roberts asserts:

> The God of Moses, the God of the Exodus, has been real to Black people. This God is one of deliverance from bondage. The God who assures the Israelites constantly, 'As I was with Moses, so I will be with thee' has comforted, strengthened, and brought great assurance to Black Christians throughout all their years of oppression in [the United States].
>
> Thus the God of the Exodus is [the God of Black people]. (Roberts *Liberation and Reconciliation: A Black Theology* p. 99).

Black theology emerged formally at the end of the 1960s when impacts of the dissimilar legacies of Malcolm X and Martin King radically sharpened theological endorsement of Black power by Black clergy. Radical Black clergy found the Christianity of the racist White church oppressive. They found intolerable contradictions between White supremacy and Christianity and concluded that Black power was justified in the providence of a God of liberation. In order to support a theology of Black power, radical Black clergy studied the history of the Black church, invisible and visible. Immediately evident from their studies was the *essential paradigmatic significance of Exodus for their theological views*. Slave spirituals, testimonies and sermons and political manifestoes of educated clergy and laity like Henry H. Garnet and David Walker were established as essential sources for Black theology. Indeed, Walker wrote in his classic *Appeal* that God '... being a just and holy being will one day appear fully in behalf of the oppressed, and arrest the progress of the avaricious oppressors ...' (Walker *Appeal* p. 3). Walker's understanding of God's partiality to the oppressed is a product of his understanding of Exodus. Walker, moreover, agitated for the violent overthrow of slavery. Reading Walker, then, Black theologians discovered that the historical character of Exodus led many of their ancestors to fight to the death for liberation. Henry Highland Garnet's interpretation of the Exodus is especially intriguing:

> If you must bleed, let it all come at once—rather *die freeman, than live to be the slaves*. It is impossible like the children of Israel, to make a grand Exodus from the land of bondage. The Pharaohs are on both sides of the blood red waters! (John H. Bracey Jr., *et al. Black Nationalism in America* p. 73).

Garnet here is not rejecting the Exodus as an archetype of God's sensitivity to the oppressed. Rather he wishes to make it clear that God, as a God of liberation, has sanctified insurrection. He writes to the slaves: 'It is in your power so to torment the God-cursed slaveholders, that they will be glad to let you go free. ... Yes the tyrants would meet with plagues more terrible than those of Pharaoh' (*ibid.* p. 75). His theodicy, then, was elucidated in resistance to slavery's advocates.

In sum, faith in a personal God of liberation has not only assured Blacks of inheritance of heaven, but also fuelled their fires of revolt. Insurrections, running away, emigration and support of the Union all suggest that slaves' interpretation of Exodus inspired resistance. Denmark Vesey's revolt bore intriguing relation to his understanding of post-Exodus events (Gayraud Wilmore *Black Religion And Black Radicalism* p. 58). Harriet Tubman's recurrent sojourns 'way down into slavery land' earned her the title of Moses among the slaves. Lincoln's army progression into the south was heralded in the slaves quarters with song: 'I am bound for the promised land ...' (Miles M. Fisher *Negro Slave Songs in the United States* p. 156). Henry Mcneal Turner's call to return to 'Guinea' pulled in its train the Black slave belief that Canaan, the promised land, was Africa (*ibid.* p. 45). That Exodus today, then, is an essential archetype for Black theologians' focus on liberation marks the extension of a radical Black Christian tradition into the late twentieth century.

Like their forebears, radical Black theologians state unambiguously, Exodus reveals that *liberation is this-worldly*. Thus James Cone, who has the distinction of textually bringing this radical Black Christian tradition of liberation and protest to fruition as *Black* theology, writes:

> It is important to note the history in which God chose to grant a self-disclosure. It was granted to an oppressed people, and the nature of the revelatory deed was synonymous with the emancipation of that people. The Exodus of Israel from Egypt was a revelation-liberation event. In this revelatory event, Israel came to know God as the liberator of the oppressed, and also realised that its being as a people was inseparable from divine concomitance. Thus Yahweh was known primarily for deeds done for Israel when other political powers threatened its existence as a community (Cone *A Black Theology Of Liberation* 2nd. ed. p. 47).

Thus for Cone, as for Walker and Garnet, '... God's revelation means political emancipation' (*ibid.*). God is a God of *liberation on earth as well as a God of redemption in heaven*. Indeed, the Exodus has been for Black Christians a most familiar theopolitical idiom. Analogically, Black Christian freedom fighters have been understood as Moses; White oppressors, as Pharaoh. Dr King in his mountaintop speech obviously likened himself to Moses (*Martin Luther King, Jr.: A Documentary ... Montgomery To Memphis* ed. Flip Schulke p. 224). King, moreover, in relating his faith that 'interposition and nullification' is penultimately defeated in God's providence, alludes to the drowning of Pharaoh's army. 'The meaning of this story', King writes, 'is not found in the drowning of the Egyptian soldiers, for no one should rejoice at the death or defeat of a human being. Rather, this story symbolises the death of evil and of inhuman oppression and unjust exploitation' (King *Strength to Love* p. 78). For King and Black theologians, the drowning of Pharaoh symbolises the justice of God. Drawing on the history of radical Black Christianity, then, Black theologians' usage of the Exodus is intrinsic to their doctrine of God. Roberts implies as much as he writes:

> The exodus is ... paradigmatic of God's manner of acting in history and throughout creation. In the light of this event, the creator and liberator of Israel is affirmed as the creator of the world and Lord of history (Roberts *A Black Political Theology* p. 28).

For Black theologians, a doctrine which ignores that God is not only creator, but also liberator, is moribund.

2. WEEP NO MORE MARY: CANAAN IS THE LAND FOR ME

I would like now further to explore doctrinal implications of the Exodus as a theological paradigm with unique significance to Black theologians. Discussion of the Exodus as a paradigm of Black theology necessitates *discussion of Jesus*. As Professor Cone explains: '... the God of Israelite history ... is the God revealed in Jesus Christ ...' (Cone *Liberation* p. 1). If the Exodus has been the paradigm for Black theologians' belief in the liberating God of Moses, then Jesus has given that belief increased existential power. It should be clear by now that Black theologians partly trace that historic sensibility to slave religion, which is quite appropriate. What better way to understand the Exodus as a paradigm for Black theology than as an expression of the religion of former slaves? Black theologians' interpretation of Jesus' passion has led to their conviction that their slave ancestors, more than Whites who proselytised the slaves, were justified in Christ, sanctified, and thus elected to ultimate salvation and penultimate liberation. Thus Black theologians claim to have the most authentically Christian theology. 'There can be no Christian theology', writes Cone, 'that is not identified unreservedly with those who are humiliated and abused' (*ibid.*). Theology, for Black theologians like Cone, is most Christian when it emerges from the context of the oppressed. Thus in making Exodus paradigmatic, the faith of the slaves, more than the writings of the Church fathers of the patristic period, is tradition for Black theologians.

Part of that tradition is the *spirituals of the slaves*. In certain spirituals, slaves reveal their perception of the proximity of their suffering to Jesus'. Professor Cone explains: '... slaves knew the significance of the pain and shame of Jesus' death on the cross [and] they found themselves by his side' (Cone *The Spirituals and the Blues* p. 53). In their eschatological imagination, the reciprocity between the salvific past and the redemptive present allowed them to transcend spatio-temporal limitations, placing them at the foot of the cross. There, they told Jesus' mother:

Oh Mary, don't you weep, don't you moan,
Oh Mary, don't you weep, don't you moan,
Pharaoh's army got drownded,
Oh, Mary don't you weep.

The slaves in that spiritual relate: the awesome events of the Exodus and the resurrection; the archetype of liberation and the prototype of the ultimate liberated person; the God of liberation and the Son of that God who was their brother in suffering. The Exodus, for many slaves, was but the sign of the inevitability of the resurrection. Developing this insight, Black theologians claim that the resurrection has brought to eschatological fruition the promise enshrined in the covenant of Sinai. Roberts puts it this way:

> The exodus provides a central category for interpreting not only the Old Testament but the work of Jesus. ... The exodus was an event in which people experienced unexpected deliverance from bondage ... and meant the opening up of an until-then impossible future for those who had been oppressed. (*Reconciliation* p. 29).

In short, the impact of the faith of the slaves has led Black theologians to intrinsically *relate Jesus to the Yahweh of the Exodus*. Both Persons reveal the judgment of God on chattelisation and victimisation. Thus whereas most Christians, in order to unify the Old and New Testaments, have tended to claim that Abraham foreshadows justification, the faith of Black theologians has essentially related the Exodus and the resurrection. The Exodus is the paradigm of God as a God of liberation and foreshadows God's incarnation of the *definitive* revelation of the election of the oppressed—Jesus the fellow sufferer, the Word of liberation made flesh.

It is problematic to say, slaves bequeathed to contemporary Black theologians a Christology, a doctrine of God, a soteriology and an eschatology. Nonetheless, ideas and records of the piety of slaves indicate that the Exodus and the resurrection are biblical supports from which Black theologians have uniquely constructed a doctrine of God and a Christology, both of which have eschatological significance in terms of a praxis of liberation.

Black theologians have learned from their ancestors that liberation is divinely initiated action against the oppressor. It is not that Black theologians have believed they were sinless in comparison to the Whites who have abused and exploited their people. They have simply asserted that their oppressors have in God's providence been destined to play the role requisite for victory of the truth: God is no respecter of persons. Implicitly, their doctrine of God is of Persons providentially dispensed to penultimately and ultimately institute political justice. Initial revelation of that justice occurred in events of the Exodus.

Among Black theologians, Exodus has confirmed that God has chosen blackness over whiteness in the same way that God elected the enslaved progeny of Jacob over imperial Egypt. Black theologians, then, know that their ancestors who survived the middle passage, who were unpacked and unloaded in the new world emaciated, diseased and bewildered, were persons of value. Resiliency of vestiges of their ancestral ways in their ringshouts and spirituals confirms for Black theologians that the God of Exodus was the God who pressed on their forebears a distinctive image. Although early missionaries thought it their burden to christianise Africans they believed barely evolved from lower primates, Black theologians know their ancestors have been God's chosen people. For Black theologians, God has made those who appeared to be heathen—Blacks—more holy than those who appeared to be divinely elected—Whites. That is today a seminal teaching of God in Black theology.

Professor Cone asserts insightfully that God is Black in identification with the Black oppressed. That God is Black is the Word which has become flesh in Black theology. Black christology implies the Exodus as part of a doctrine of God who both sinks Pharaoh's army and becomes one of the descendants of the slaves who crossed over into Canaan. The eschatological insight of Black slaves bears repeating: 'Don't cry Mary, Pharaoh's army drowned.' The *God* who swallowed them is identical with Jesus Christ. Pressed further, that *trinitarian insight* yields this one. The Spirit reveals blackness as *a* sign of the humanity of God. Blackness has been made spiritually fit to absorb the way, the truth and the light. God not only liberates the oppressed and afflicts the oppressor in the Exodus, God historically is 'The Oppressed One' who through the Spirit moves in history among the oppressed ones. This is the good news! Judgment is daily passed on the oppressors. To be in Christ, then, is to be in political solidarity with the oppressed. In God's grace, faith in Christ makes the theopolitical struggle for liberation from White supremacy, capitalist exploitation, imperialism and misogynism the work of the Spirit. Penultimately in God's providence, faith without works is dead. Ultimately, Pharaoh, because he is not one of the elect, drowns again. Exodus, as a paradigm for Black theology, works every time.

Oh Canaan, sweet Canaan,
I am bound for the land of Canaan.

Dianne Bergant

Exodus as a Paradigm in Feminist Theology

THE TITLE of this essay suggests that the ideas advanced develop out of a twofold perspective, i.e., biblical and feminist. One might be justified in asking: 'Is this a biblical study with feminist ramifications or a feminist interpretation of a biblical theme?' The primary focus of this investigation is the socioreligious origin of Israel as expressed in the theological symbol 'Exodus.' For this reason, one might be inclined to view it as more biblical than feminist. However, feminist concerns have predisposed me to engage in dialogue with the biblical tradition from a particular point of view and with a particular hermeneutical preference. Therefore, one can rightly call this study feminist. For myself, I find it impossible to separate the two approaches. The perspective from which this essay is written has espoused *concerns that are both biblical and feminist* without being predominantly one or the other.

Preliminary clarifications are in order. The term *Exodus* is used in several different ways in the essay. The specific meaning of each distinct use must be clear if one is to follow the development of thought. Exodus-event refers to the historical event or events which brought into existence Israel as a people. Exodus-symbol refers to the cluster of themes which constitutes the theological meaning of that historical event. 'Exodus' is used when no sharp distinction between event and symbol is intended, or when referring to the interpretive key.

1. EXODUS: HISTORICAL EVENT AND THEOLOGICAL SYMBOL

Many biblical theologians now hold a view regarding the origins of ancient Israel that has been largely confirmed and elucidated by recent sociological studies (e.g., Bright, Mendenhall, Gottwald). This view claims that Israelite origins are to be found within a *socioreligious movement of dissent and revolt*. Here we should recall that according to the prevailing mythopoetic worldview of the ancient Near East, social and religious structures were divinely ordained and eternally valid, thus, part of the primordial order. Israel, with its Yahwistic faith, was a revolt against this worldview. Whether this revolt was derived from Yahwistic faith or Yahwism was the religious symbolisation of this social struggle is a point of disagreement among scholars today. Still, for its part the biblical tradition suggests that Yahwistic faith played the prominent role in this socioreligious movement. This should not be taken as proof of the historical accuracy of the tradition, however, for a tradition may well testify more to theological interpretation than to an originating historical event.

This view of Israelite origins suggests that we might have to look at 'Exodus' quite differently. Rather than understand it primarily as deliverance from oppressive forces or structures, we might instead interpret it as the rejection of *any* force or structure, oppressive or even benevolent, that claims for itself primordial origin. Perhaps a closer look at the fundamental meaning of 'Exodus' as well as its later understandings will help to make this distinction clear.

Studies show that the *tendency to identify the deity with the prevailing political power structure* is one of the most common patterns of thought in the ancient Near East. Certain creation myths state that human beings exist to support the politicoreligious establishment (e.g., *Enuma Elish*). To challenge one's place within the structure or, what is even worse, to challenge the structure itself, is to oppose the cosmic order and the divine powers responsible for it. Such an action constitutes religious rebellion as well as social revolt.

The biblical narrative itself points to such revolt and rebellion in Israel's case. Whether it was Egyptian imperialism or Canaanite city-state feudalism that the people had thrown off, they did indeed reject their former sociopolitical structures in favour of an *egalitarian confederation*. In fact, the laws that governed tribal and intertribal relationships forbade anything that might lead to the subjection of one free Israelite to another. Whatever hierarchy was allowed existed only for the sake of service to rather than domination of other Israelites. The strong opposition to the establishment of the monarchy (see 1 Sam. 8) clearly suggests that resistance to hierarchic power structures was deeply rooted in the self-consciousness of the people. When the monarchy was finally legitimated, it was only with the assurance that the monarch was to be considered first and foremost one of the people, subject to the law like everyone else (see 2 Sam. 7).

It now seems quite clear that just as the religions of Egypt and Canaanite city-states served the purposes of imperialism and feudalism, so the tribal religion of Israel served egalitarian interests. *Yahwism clearly opposed class privileges* that would exempt one from social responsibility. The prophets' condemnations give ample evidence of this. The Sabbath rest, the Sabbatical year, and the Year of Jubilee were all attempts at creating and recreating a society within which the production and consumption of goods and the basic enjoyment of life could be shared by all.

The Exodus-symbol may well have had its roots in this historical experience of social revolt and religious rebellion. *However, within the biblical tradition its meaning is principally theological.* Here it represents God's deliverance of Israel from Egyptian oppression. Since the socioreligious body that emerged from the Exodus-event was structured according to the ethical demands of a covenantal law that was egalitarian in nature, there was no reason to focus on the original revolutionary character of the Exodus-event. The symbol never functioned as an incentive to revolution because the egalitarian nature of the society made it less apt to be oppressive. Instead, it functioned as an incentive to fidelity to the covenant and its obligations (see Leviticus 25:42; Micah 6:3–4). God had delivered Israel from foreign oppression and made Israel a 'chosen people'. In its turn, Israel was to be true to its election and obedient to its egalitarian constitution. The Exodus-symbol served to remind Israel of its beginnings and of its responsibilities. Through the ages both Jewish and Christian communities have understood events in history and in individual lives in terms of this symbol. It has become the primary paradigm for theologies of liberation.

2. EXODUS: INTERPRETIVE KEY

Besides serving as a theological symbol, 'Exodus' can also function as an *interpretive key to critique any theological articulation, paradigm or symbol that claims to be divinely ordained and eternally valid.* A closer look at the traditioning process that gave birth to the scriptures will show that traditions were quite flexible not only during the period of their formation but also as they were interpreted. Their revelatory character was believed to reside not so much in the form they took as in the witness they gave to God's continuing involvement in the world. The importance of the form is not to be denied, but form is subordinate to the power of witness. For example, the particular symbols of God's active involvement in the midst of the people which were so characteristic of tribal religion had to be reinterpreted and reshaped as Israel embraced the monarchy with its State religion. The same kind of radical reinterpretation of tradition took place after the exile as Israel reconstituted itself as a socioreligious entity in its own land. On this level, then, 'Exodus' can be seen as a *fundamental key to radical reinterpretation.*

As an interpretive key, 'Exodus' opens the way to whole new worlds of meaning. As a symbol to be interpreted, it provides the way of entering those worlds. Even a cursory examination of the Exodus-symbol, as it appears in those passages that testify to the Exodus-event, will uncover elements of the core of that tradition. There we see God revealed as (*a*) particularly concerned with the oppressed and mistreated, (*b*) accompanying them in their movements, (*c*) and leading them into the future toward *šālôm*. This core tradition can function as the basis of an interpretive approach.

First, the prominent theme of God's concern for the *oppressed and mistreated*, which is given expression in covenantal law, suggests the basic egalitarian emphasis of the tradition. This further suggests that the message of the text (the focus of most contemporary literary critical methods), the community from which the text arose (the focus of historical reconstructive methods), and the context of the interpreter (contemporary life experience and the customary ways of understanding) must be critiqued from an egalitarian point of view.

In addition to this, conviction that *God accompanies the people in their movements* transfers the context of revelation from the cosmic plane to the realm of history. While historical critical methods seek to discover the earliest testimonies to the revelation of God, a dynamic historical consciousness leads to an appreciation of the revelatory possibilities of the present moment.

Finally, commitment to *a God who leads the people forward toward šālôm*, or fullness of being, redirects attention from the static categories of the past to challenging possibilities of the future. The meaning of a tradition is not confined to past or even present meanings. The future holds an as yet unexplored treasury of meaning.

In summary, then, an egalitarian critique, a dynamic historical consciousness, and an openness to a 'surplus of meaning' constitute the basis of an interpretive approach based on 'Exodus.'

3. FEMINISM: CRITIQUE OF PREUNDERSTANDING

The interpretive approach outlined above may well be biblical, but is it feminist? Concern for the oppressed and mistreated, recognition of God's action in history, and openness to the future are foundational to many contemporary interpretive approaches. Where does one find a *specifically feminist dimension in this approach?*

One of the most fundamental insights of contemporary interpretive theory is the acknowledgment of the operative presence of *preunderstandings*. When we go to the text we are not free of the traditions that have shaped our worldview. These traditions have predisposed our judgments, called forth our values, and actually shaped the way we perceive reality. Our culture has played a very active part in forming us into the people we have become. We possess the features of that culture and we carry the effects of its history.

Our preunderstanding is never fully self-conscious. We are not always aware of the ways in which our traditions promote our well-being and enhance our lives. It is usually in situations where we feel restricted that we begin to question the appropriateness, even the justice, first of the situation and then of its underlying presuppositions. This explains why those who suffer oppression or who are relegated to marginality or invisibility within a society are better critics of that society than are those who are privileged and satisfied. It is here that *feminism acts as an indispensable critique of preunderstanding*.

Feminist critique operates on *many different levels*. It sensitises us to language and imagery that explicitly insult, subtly minimise, or completely disregard women. It alerts us to situations in which women are relegated to tasks that are always subordinate and exclusively auxiliary. It challenges presuppositions that flow from an anthropology that is androcentric and mysogynist. It is the women's experience of restriction and confinement that determines the scope of this critique, for they are the ones who experience as limitation this dimension of the preunderstanding. Because the text we are interpreting may be labouring under the same limited and limiting presuppositions, the language, human experience and anthropological understanding of the text must also be critiqued from a feminist perspective.

4. FEMINISM: AGENDA FOR DIALOGUE

Interpretation has frequently been compared to dialogue with a text in order to arrive at an understanding of the text as well as of ourselves. Feminism functions in a very significant way in setting the agenda for this dialogue. It is *women's experience of restriction and confinement that determines the subject matter of this agenda*. The deep convictions that are brought to the dialogue spring from feminist consciousness and feminist critique. While they act as negative limits (since whatever contradicts these convictions cannot be accepted) their interpretations challenge us to new ways of perceiving and living.

The following list does not presume to be complete. Other feminists might draw up a very different list. Nor does it claim to be an exclusively feminist agenda. It is merely a sampling of deep convictions reached by means of a feminist critique of women's experience of restriction and confinement. Reflecting on their own experience should open women to a concern for the struggles of other people who are similarly restricted and confined and who share the same agenda.

Relationship to be Fostered

Collaboration	(in reaction to)	arbitrary control
cooperation	(in reaction to)	competition
interdependence	(in reaction to)	independence/dependence
respect	(in reaction to)	disdain
compassion	(in reaction to)	indifference
justice	(in reaction to)	exploitation
mutuality	(in reaction to)	domination/subjugation
harmony	(in reaction to)	offensiveness/defensiveness

The Exodus-symbol, as the basis of the interpretive approach, and feminism, as the perspective within which it functions, make critical demands on each other. The egalitarian point of view of the symbol calls to account feminism's critique of preunderstanding as well as the agenda that it brings to the dialogue. In turn, the deep convictions that spring from feminist consciousness and feminist critique call to account the content of the core tradition.

5. EXODUS AS A PARADIGM IN FEMINIST THEOLOGY

The interpretive approach advanced in this essay may enable us to address certain biblical issues, but it does not directly answer the question of canon. Neither the traditioning process itself nor the traditions as they were undergoing the process were declared canonical. It was the final product, the text, that became canonical scriptures. Given the pervasively patriarchal and androcentric nature of these scriptures, can one honestly look upon them as bearers of revelation?

Here it may help to recall that *revelation is an experience of disclosure*. This experience of disclosure is followed by a search for the meaning of the disclosure, a meaning which is then articulated in testimony. The testimony can take various forms of theological discourse, the collection of which is known as scripture. *The biblical tradition, then, is not itself the revelation but is a testimony to revelation*. It is, in fact, steps removed from the revelatory experience. This does not detract from its importance, but situates it properly.

Is disclosure confined to an experience of the past? Our tradition, both the formative process (*traditio*) and the fruits of that process (*traditum*) answer in the negative. Traditions were shaped and reshaped until they achieved the form that has come down to us, and the content of these traditions testifies to revelatory experiences throughout the history of the people. But even this explanation brings us up against the question of canonisation. Does the closed canon mean the cessation of the traditioning process? And does a canonical text restrict the meaning of the disclosure to an articulation that is not only culturally conditioned but discriminatory and oppressive?

As stated above, a text, even a canonical text, is only an articulation of a testimony; it is not the revelation. Its canonical claim asserts that the *meaning* of the articulated tradition is normative for the believing community, not the *form*. For example, Exodus 14 and 15 both testify to the Exodus-event. One is narrative discourse, the other is poetic. Both texts are canonical articulations of testimonies that witness to the same meaning of the revelatory event. A specific genre may be vital for a particular discourse, but that discourse is still only a testimony to the meaning of the disclosure. When the revelatory event to which the testimonies bear witness is cherished as the founding event of the community, (the event that forged their identity as a people in relationship with God), those articulated traditions that are regarded as authentic expressions of the basic self-understanding of the people are considered normative. To repeat, it is the meaning of the tradition that is normative, not the form.

This would suggest that a closed canon does not mean the cessation of the traditioning process. It simply means that new articulations will not be considered canonical. Nor does a canonical text restrict the meaning of the disclosure to an articulation that is not only culturally conditioned but discriminatory and oppressive. Divine self-disclosure is polysemic. Here again 'Exodus' functions as an interpretive key. *It stands in opposition to what is discriminatory and oppressive*; it affirms the promise of new and life-giving things to come; and it attests to the revelatory possibilities of the present moment.

The interpreter of Scripture engages in dialogue with the meaning of a tradition that is articulated in some form of theological discourse. The feminist both critiques the tradition and the contemporary context and then focuses the direction of the dialogue. The Christian opens up to the dialogue's possibilities of both personal and social transformation.

PART IV

Evaluation and Hermeneutical Conclusions

Gregory Baum

Exodus Politics

1. RADICAL RELIGION

THE WESTERN radical tradition, though largely secular in spirit, is *linked to biblical symbols of redemption mediated by the Christian religion.* Biblical symbols of deliverance have also been handed on by Jewish religion. While Marx himself had little awareness of the radical element in the religious tradition, his followers became increasingly conscious of the affinity between certain religious movements of the past and the emerging Socialist movement. Friedrich Engels wrote essays on early Christianity in which he interpreted the Jesus movement as an expression of class struggle in the first century. Engels also studied Thomas Muenzer and the Peasant War of 1524. Again he interpreted the religious language used by Christian radicals as a strategic disguise for their this-wordly, subversive political aims.[1] It became quite common for Marxists to write books on early Christianity, books that are completely dated today, in which they offered a one-sidedly political interpretation of Christ's mission.[2]

In 1921, Ernst Bloch, an original and independent Marxist, published his *Thomas Muenzer als Theologe der Revolution*, in which he examined the sermons of this Christian radical and concluded, against Engels and other Marxist interpreters, that the religious language used was not a disguise for secular political aims but an eloquent expression of deeply felt religious experiences, experiences that related Muenzer and his followers to their God and at the same time urged them to political commitment. Here genuine religious experiences, mediated by certain biblical themes, had radical political meaning.

Karl Mannheim, a sociologist who did not regard himself as a Marxist, published his famous *Ideology and Utopia* in 1929, in which he examined the impact of ideas, symbols and stories on political history. In a chapter entitled 'The Utopian Mentality', Mannheim examined what he regarded as the *major utopian ideas that have affected Western history*. The first one of these, according to Mannheim, was the revolutionary vision of the millennarian movements that intermittently emerged in the late middle ages right up to Thomas Muenzer and the radical Anabaptists. These movements, nourished by religious experiences of people from the oppressed strata, generated what Mannheim regarded as the beginning of 'politics in the modern sense', that is politics understood as 'the more or less conscious participation of all strata of society in the achievement of some mundane purpose'.[3]

While some scholars think that the historical connection between utopian Christian movements and subsequent secular radicalism reveals how deeply the revolutionary tradition is rooted in the spiritual heritage of the West, there are other scholars for whom this connection reveals the tragic flaw of Western radicalism and explains the arrival of political totalitarianism on the right and on the left in the twentieth century. Norman Cohn's *The Pursuit of the Millenium*, first published in 1957, offers a detailed historical analysis of the millennarian movements of the late middle ages to the radical Anabaptists, including an appendix on the Ranters in Cromwell's England. The author concludes that all of these groups operated out of the same utopian vision. They expected the coming of God's judgment on their wicked society, they saw themselves as holy remnants and as instruments of God's wrath, and they expected the arrival of God's kingdom, the new covenant, the promised land, in the near future. While some groups believed that this kingdom of peace and justice would last a thousand years until the final parousia, others believed that God's peaceable kingdom on earth would have no end. At certain historical moments, these movements, inspired by their leaders, regarded themselves as the destroyers of society in God's name and the builders of the new Jerusalem. According to Norman Cohn this political messianism lacked rationality, it engendered fanatical devotion and produced unreal expectations, it always led to self-righteousness, contempt and brutal behaviour toward the enemy, and usually ended up in dictatorship. 'It is such a view of history, at once teleological and cataclysmic,' Cohn writes, 'that has been presupposed and invoked alike by the millennarian movements described in the present study and by the great totalitarian movements of our own day.'[4] This similarity includes the paranoia and megalomania of the charismatic leaders. By implication Cohn accuses the entire Western revolutionary tradition of operating out of a messianic imagination that despite its high ideals again and again *produced unreal expectations, fanatical*

devotion, irrational behaviour, dictatorial regimes and ruthless repression or
elimination of the enemy.

The far reaching implications of *The Pursuit of the Millennium* have been
criticised by several scholars. A recent book, *Exodus and Revolution*, by the
well-known political scientist Michael Walzer, offers an *important corrective
of Norman Cohn's thesis.* Walzer admits that political messianism associated
with the millennarian movements has produced the sad results ascribed to
them by Cohn. But as a student of Western revolution Walzer argues that the
revolutions were indeed guided by a social imagination derived from the Bible,
especially the Exodus story, but they avoided the messianic expectations of the
millennarians. It is of course possible to assimilate the Exodus into the
apocalyptical imagination of the millennarians. This was in fact done by the
great millennarian preachers. But it is also possible, Walzer insists, to read the
Exodus story as *an alternative* to the millennarian imagination.

Walzer offers a careful reading of the biblical account of the Exodus that
brings to light the political symbols important to Western revolutionaries, and
he contrasts them with the apocalypticism of millennarians and other political
messianists. Walzer speaks approvingly of 'Exodus politics' in contrast with
millennarian irrationality. In his book Walzer expresses his admiration for
Latin American Liberation Theology because it refuses to read the Exodus
story in line with messianic expectations and eschatological fulfillment.[5]
For Liberation Theology, Walzer notes, *the new society is never equated
with the kingdom of God.* The Exodus story invites revolutionaries to a
political imagination that remains within the rational possibilities of their
history.

The central point of Walzer is that the Exodus story as told refers to a
worldly movement within time and space. It is not part of a cosmic journey. In
Egypt the people suffered from oppression that is clearly described in political
terms. In the desert, the people underwent several trials, many of them fell
away, until they were united in the same political vision and purpose. And in
the promised land the people sought the freedoms of which they were deprived
in Egypt, not the Garden of Eden. The Exodus story reports the *struggle of a
people for a social existence that is possible within the concrete conditions of
their history.* The presence of God in this story in no way removes the
historical realism. Throughout his book Walzer contrasts this reading of the
Exodus with the expectations of the millennarians for whom the oppression in
the land of bondage was not simply political but included the entire alienation
from which they suffered, and for whom the promised land was not simply a
place of greater justice but the New Jerusalem, the place of total redemption.
The millennarian vision pointed *beyond the possibilities of history.*

Walzer examines the Exodus story in four chapters, the land of bondage, the murmuring in the desert, the covenant of a free people, and the promised land.

2. EXODUS AND REVOLUTION

In the description of the enslavement in Egypt, the *biblical text remains historically specific*. The people suffer under slavery. Their oppression is not chattel slavery. The people have come to Egypt as guest workers who later found themselves forced to work for the government under conditions of great deprivation. The people suffer from political tyranny and material misery. The clear distinction between political and economic oppression, introduced by political scientists like Hannah Arendt, is not validated in the case of Egypt. In fact, the Exodus story makes one sceptical in regard to the political opinion that presents political oppression as intolerable totalitarianism while evaluating economic oppression as more benign and hence as calling for greater patience. The biblical designation of the Israelites in Egypt as 'the poor and the oppressed', intertwining the economic and political elements, has entered into the literature of the Western revolutionary tradition. Moreover, the liberation of the Israelites as projected in the covenant legislation was defined precisely as the overcoming of the twofold domination they experienced in Egypt: *bread in the context of dignity and freedom.*

Walzer notes that the biblical story does not look upon Pharaoh as a devil or the incarnation of evil. Pharaoh is a man, limited in his power, not linked symbolically to all that is evil in the world. The people are angry at him, they are often afraid of him, and yet they hope that they can escape from his power. In no way do they look upon him as a representation of cosmic evil, to which they must submit in patience.

The passage to the promised land goes through the wilderness. There is no ecstatic entry into liberation. The *passage takes time, it involves conflict, it includes failures, it generates crises, it slowly educates the people.* In particular, the biblical text describes the divided consciousness of the people. On the one hand, they long for liberation, they are ready for the new experiment of freedom; on the other hand, they realise the many sacrifices that will have to be made and hence they often dream of their safer existence in Egypt. Why do they still hanker after Egypt? This question has been asked again and again in revolutionary movements. It would seem that the symbols of power and prestige of the rulers have been internalised by the oppressed. The Israelites in the desert remember 'when we sat by the fleshpots and ate bread to the full'. In fact, the oppressed could afford only the bread, but they sat near the fleshpots of the Egyptians, smelled the aroma, and dreamt that they could be like the

Egyptians and eat from those pots. Yet the same people cry unto God. Their cry reveals that they have not fully internalised the dreams of their oppressors. They cry to God because they realise that something is terribly wrong. They want to be delivered.

The Exodus story deals with many of the debates that have gone on in revolutionary movements. Some biblical passages speak of the Exodus as the work of Moses, or God's work through Moses, a free gift to the people of Israel, while other passages declare that the people themselves are involved in their deliverance, it is their responsibility, it depends ultimately on their fidelity. Is revolution a social movement managed from above through gifted political leaders? Or is it a people's movement from below? Or is the movement sound only if there is a constant interaction between top and bottom?

The biblical account can be read in *two different ways*. It is possible to put the emphasis on Moses' decision to punish the worshippers of the golden calf. He asked the Levites to slay the unfaithful. He appealed not to the recognised magistrates but to a group of volunteers to execute the purge. Walzer calls this the *Leninist reading of the text*. All revolutions have punished the unfaithful, they all have had their purges, usually brought about by groups of volunteers. Since English Canada was largely founded by Empire Loyalists fleeing from the American Revolution it is not surprising the Canadian history books put a good deal of emphasis on the purges, on the harassment, persecution and killings to which the people loyal to the British Crown (about 20 per cent of the population) were subjected during the American Revolutionary War.

There is, however, another reading of the Exodus story, one that emphasised the long march through the desert, the new law given to the people, and the education to which they were exposed. What went on in the desert was a spiritual transformation. Here the backsliding is corrected not by purges but by conversion, education and liturgical rites. There is hope that the new generation which does not know Egypt and whose minds have not been affected by the Egyptian dream will be more faithful to the revolutionary ideal. Walzer calls this the *social democratic reading of the biblical text*. Here Moses is not seen as the man of power, the charismatic leader who must be obeyed at all costs. Here Moses finds his authority challenged: 'Who has made you a prince over us?' (Num. 16:13).

The covenant in the desert takes account of the *ambiguity of the people's commitment to liberation*. What is demanded, therefore, is the endorsement of the covenant by all the people, men, women and children. The commitment of the leaders is not enough. The people must be engaged in the new social order, and they must renew this commitment every year. The new society is possible only if the people continue to commit themselves to the ideal of freedom. A collective engagement of this kind has always been the aim of revolution. It has hardly ever been easy. Walzer recalls that Calvin wanted the endorsement of the covenant by the whole population of Geneva, but he had to send the police to gather the people in front of the cathedral.

Related to this is the *conditional character of the Mosaic covenant*. While God's covenant with Abraham, and prior to that with Noah, was unilateral and unconditional, the Mosaic covenant is bilateral and qualified. Only if the people remain faithful to the terms of the covenant is God obliged to fulfil his side of the pact. In fact, if the people choose to become unfaithful they are liable to be punished. The emphasis is here on the freedom and dignity of the participants. While occasionally we read that as the people were 'slaves' of Pharaoh so they shall now be 'slaves' of Yahweh and that this slavery shall make them free, the main emphasis of the biblical text, Walzer argues, is on the free participation of the people. In the radical literature of the West, the *covenant has always been the great model for popular involvement*.

Through the covenant the people become holy. Their Torah introduces them to a life removed from the injustices inflicted upon them in Egypt. Their new law institutionalises the repudiation of the Egyptian bondage. There shall be no rulers lording it over the people, there shall be no slave group at the bottom, no poor people exposed to misery; there shall be protection for the weak, sharing of resources, and respect given to all and each. The people are holy when they tolerate no return to Egypt.

The *rationality of the new legislation*, Walzer argues, distinguishes revolutionary movements from protest movements inspired by despair and irrational hope, movements that if successful, easily turn into chaos.

And what is the promised land in the biblical story? It is *not paradise*. It is modestly described as the land where milk and honey flows. No fleshpots there. Other biblical passages clarify that milk and honey refers to an agricultural society where people own their plot of land, produce the food they need, and work for themselves, where people have their dignity respected and have no princes over them (Deut. 8:7–9, Isa. 65:21–22). Milk and honey is therefore not merely material: it is at the same time spiritual, it refers to freedom and dignity.

3. EXODUS POLITICS

In his analysis of political messianism, Walzer is as critical as Cohn. Walzer offers *two characteristics of the millennarian spirit*. First, millennarians long for an *apocalyptical event*, a violent moment of history, out of which is to emerge a gratuitous condition of peace and harmony. Exodus politics, on the other hand, is aware of the ambiguity of people's consciousness, it makes its plans within the possibilities of history, it is rational, it is satisfied with partial solutions. And secondly, millennarians yearn for the last day, they *want to force the end.* The worse the better. Every struggle is for them the last battle, their enemies are satan or anti-Christ, and their victory will be ultimate redemption. In Exodus politics, on the contrary, the ultimate is not an appropriate category. The end in view is liberation, but concretely and modestly defined, never a state free of temptations, reversals and contradictions. In this context Walzer mentions with satisfaction Gutierrez' arguments against political messianism.[6]

Walzer's argument is persuasive. He is able to back up his interpretation of Exodus politics with references to revolutionaries who have actually used the biblical text in their struggle. The author's reading of the Exodus story has one weakness which he recognises himself. He pays no attention to the biblical report of the conquest of the promised land, accompanied as it was by military cruelty and God's command to kill the interfering tribes, men, women and children. This report has been used by political leaders who sought in the Bible a guide for the struggle for liberation or simply for victory. Yet Walzer argues that in the subsequent Jewish and Christian traditions, these harsh passages have been regarded as curious remnants of an older imagination, at odds with the non-oppression theme of the covenant.

Walzer is committed to Exodus politics. He thinks that the Exodus continues to have much to teach us about the meaning and possibility of radical politics and about its proper form. However, when he summarises this lesson on the last page of his book, he fails—and in fact *contradicts himself.* This is how he sums up the lesson: 'First, that wherever we live, it is probably Egypt; second, that there is a better place, a world more attractive, a promised land; and third, that the way to the land is through the wilderness. There is no way to get from here to there except by joining together and marching.'[7]

This concluding sentence, I wish to argue, contradicts the antecedent analysis. Exodus politics demands that one does *not* designate every situation of injustice as Egypt. The house of bondage in the Exodus story is characterised by an intertwining of political and economic domination that affected every aspect of people's lives and ground them down to utter weariness. In the biblical account, a sober analysis justifies the use of the categories, 'oppressor' and 'oppressed'. It seems imperative to me that in every single situation, in every existing social conflict in history, a rational investigation must decide whether the *oppressor/oppressed category is analytically appropriate* or whether it is necessary to look for another sociological paradigm. A false application of Exodus language has devastating consequences. Because of the great suffering inflicted on people today in so many parts of the world there is a tendency, often endorsed quite uncritically, to interpret all social plights in terms of oppressor/oppressed categories.

It seems to me that the tragic conflict in Northern Ireland between the Catholic population, mainly working class, and the Protestant working class (the Protestant middle class tends to be ready for the sharing of power) must not be interpreted in terms of oppressor and oppressed. Both sides in this bloody conflict are the poor and powerless. What is needed instead is a political analysis that will allow the two sides to recognise their unequal situation as the consequence of a system, now largely of the past, that separated them and harmed them both, a political analysis that generates joint policies that promise to ameliorate the lot of both groups. The conflict between Israelis and Palestinians, it seems to me, must not be analysed in terms of oppressor/oppressed. What we have here are two discarded peoples struggling to survive out of different histories of suffering, with instruments of power that reveal the lack of symmetry of their respective pasts. What has to be found is a political paradigm that facilitates concession, compromise, dialogue and cooperation. My third example is Quebec's struggle for independence. Before the 1980 referendum on Quebec sovereignty, the Catholic bishops issued a pastoral letter in which they defended Quebec's right to self-determination but refused to advise the people whether to determine their future within Canada or whether to opt for independence. The one thing the bishops demanded was that neither side in this conflict use divine revelation to bolster its cause.[8] What does this mean? It would be unacceptable to say that Canadian unity is God's will and that Christians must therefore reject Quebec sovereignty as it would be unacceptable to say that Quebec's relatively disadvantaged position in Canada resembles that of the Israelites in Egypt and that Christians must therefore vote for exodus and Quebec sovereignty.

In his book, *God-Wrestling*, Arthur Waskow, a political scientist and religious thinker, proposed the idea that there is a paradigm for contemporary politics in the Bible that is as important or even more important than the Exodus story, namely the *conflict and reconciliation between two brothers*.[9] Waskow suggests that we read the stories of Isaac and Ishmael, and of Jacob and Esau as political paradigms. The unjust distribution of privilege between the brothers is due to decisions not their own, that may have been sinful but cannot now be wholly undone: what is available to them are gestures of admission and recognition, at first from a distance, gestures that may ultimately lead to concession and reconciliation. No political scientist, as far as I know, has studied the biblical paradigm of the two brothers to clarify its political potential.

Notes

1. Friedrich Engels *Marx & Engels on Religion* introd. by Reinhold Niehbuhr (New York 1964) p. 103.

2. See the introduction of Karl Kautsky's *Foundations of Christianity*.

3. Karl Mannheim *Ideology and Utopia* (New York 1969) p. 212.

4. Norman Cohn *The Pursuit of the Millennium* (London 1957) p. 307.

5. Michael Walzer *Exodus and Revolution* (New York 1985) p. 79.

6. *Ibid.* p. 167.

7. *Ibid.* p. 149.

8. John Williams *Canadian Churches and Social Justice* (Toronto 1984) p. 186.

9. Arthur Waskow *God-Wrestling* (New York 1978).

David Tracy

Exodus: Theological Reflection

THERE IS no paradigm *more central to Judaism than Exodus and Sinai.* The
history of the reception of this great paradigm by the rabbinic commentators
to Jewish theologians and other scholars, writers, and activists today is at the
heart of the Jewish tradition. It is possible to read Genesis as the story of
individuals and families in relationship to God. But the story of Exodus—the
classic narrative of bondage in Egypt, the promised land, the murmurings in
the wilderness, the covenant at Sinai, the leadership of Moses and Aaron, the
struggle for a better life in the promised land—is the story of a *people*. It is the
heart of the Hebrew Scriptures. Exodus is the story which the great prophets
retell and develop in and for later times. It is that story which the development
of Messianism and later apocalyptic and wisdom traditions try either to
radicalise or deflect from its centrality to the whole Bible. The great narrative
of Exodus as told in the books of Exodus, Deuteronomy, and Numbers is the
narrative of a people who have been called to struggle in the wilderness and
have been promised a new convenant and a new land but not paradise: a
realistic, this worldly promise, this promise of a better land in Canaan to
become a liberated people, Israel. The history of Jewish thought and Jewish
existence as the people of the Covenant is the history of the memory and life of
the event and texts of Exodus.

There is also no paradigm that should be *more central to Christian self-
understanding than Exodus.* At least when Christians remain faithful to their
Jewish roots Exodus becomes central to their consciousness. For it is Exodus
which provides a proper context for understanding the great Christian
paradigm of the life—ministry—death—and resurrection of Jesus Christ. In a
sense, this Christian paradigm—with its many contexts from Old Testament
traditions of Messianism, wisdom, and apocalyptic—is most faithful to itself

when it does not allow the de-historicising and de-politicising of Jesus Christ. Christianity is most itself when it is an Exodus religion.

The rise of political theology, liberation theology, and feminist theology in our period shows the re-emergence of the paradigm of Exodus as the central context (with its covenant of Sinai and its reinterpretations by the great prophets) for understanding the central text and event of Christian reality—the ministry, life and message, death and resurrection of Jesus the Christ. When Christian self-understanding is tempted to de-politicise its self-understanding and praxis anew, Christians need only reflect on Exodus as the paradigm which should inform and transform the highly personal but not individualist Christian self-understanding in the reality of the death and resurrection of Jesus Christ. When Christian theology is tempted to flee to other-worldly theology, it is able to turn to neo-Platonism and even to some strands of the Wisdom traditions of both Testaments. But it cannot turn to Exodus. For Exodus demands a resolutely *this-worldly spirituality* as it demands an historical and political, not a private or individualist understanding of Christian salvation-as-total-liberation. Finally, when Christian theology is tempted to despair of biblical realism for its political theology one can turn to the narrative of Exodus. For Exodus disallows both millennarianism and despair.

1. NO TEXT WITHOUT HISTORY

Exodus, like any classic religious paradigm, has given rise to profound plurality and ambiguity in its reception, in both theory and practice, in religious and secular thought and practice. Jew or Christian, in their differing ways, will profoundly affirm their covenantal trust in God's actions in Exodus and their hope for divine empowerment and their realization of the demand for free human historical struggle for total liberation. A Jew or a Christian will also face the ambiguities of the reception of the paradigm of Exodus in their histories. The Hebrew Scriptures can be read as a series of sometimes complementary, sometimes conflicting interpretations of Exodus, Sinai, and Covenant. Who any longer claims to find a fully coherent 'biblical theology' in these scriptures?

As modern hermeneutics with its notion of *Wirkungsgeschichte* makes clear, *no text comes to us as purely autonomous*. It comes bearing with it the history of its former receptions in theory and practice as we come to read and understand it bearing as we do, consciously and pre-consciously, the history of the effects of the texts of Exodus and all its receptions upon us. Those receptions include all those—Jewish, Christian, secular—that have gone before us and all those in our own day. There is no honest theological way to avoid that reality nor to shirk the need to face the plurality and ambiguity of the reality of the reception of the paradigm and classic texts of Exodus in our history: from the empowerment as a people of the ancient Israelites to the fate of the Canaanites and the 'murmurers' among the Israelites themselves; from the noble struggle for political freedom by Cromwell to the fate of the Irish Catholics in his self-righteous path; from the 'noble experiment' of the New England Puritans and the fate of the natives of North America (those still misnamed 'Indians'). In our own time one cannot forget either the present noble struggle of the use of Exodus in the liberation theologies of Latin American nor the frightening use of that same paradigm for taking the 'land' and for treating Black Africans as the 'Canaanites' among some South African Reformed theologians. *Even Exodus is not an innocent text.* This reality forces all theologians to realise that theology itself must now pay greater attention in all its interpretations to the pluralistic and ambiguous reception of all its classic texts, including Exodus.

History is not only contingent: *history is interruptive.* Western history is, through and through, an interruptive narrative with no single theme and no controlling plot. To be an American, for example, can be to live with pride by participating in a noble experiment of freedom and plurality. But to be a White American is also to belong to a history, partly through one use of the Exodus symbol, that includes the near-destruction of one people (the North American Indians, the true native Americans) and the enslavement of another people (the Blacks). Not to honour the ancient Greeks as our ancestors is possible only for those who lack any sense of true greatness. But to honour and belong to the Greeks is also to recognise the interruptions in their, i.e. our, history: the role of the other as barbarian; the vindictive policies of imperialist Athens towards Melos and other colonies; the unexamined role of women and slaves in the polis; the cries of the Athenians themselves in the quarries of Syracuse.

Similarly, to claim the ancient Israelites as our predecessors or Exodus as our theme is an honour. But that claim also forces us to face the *patriarchal nature of that society.* We cannot forget what the Israelites of the Exodus did to the Canaanites and the murmurers among the Israelites and what their prayers against the children of their enemies might mean. To cherish the New Testament as a charter document of Exodus-liberation in cross and resurrection is entirely right. Yet we must also face its *anti-Judaic strands* in some of its 'new-Covenant' and 'new Exodus' language: strands which reach us with the full history of the effects of centuries of Christian 'teaching of contempt' for the Jews. And we have just begun to face the centuries of *subjugation of women* in Jewish and Christian history—indeed, in most accounts of the Exodus itself (save Deuteronomy 29:10–13).

2. AMBIGUITY

No classic text like Exodus comes to us without *the plural and history of effects of its own production and all its former receptions.* Nor does any classic event, be it the Renaissance, the Reformation or the Enlightenment—or the event Exodus. 'Every great work of civilization', as Walter Benjamin insisted, 'is at the same time a work of barbarism.' Plurality seems an adequate word to suggest the extraordinary variety which any study of language shows and any study of the variety of receptions of any classic documents. Ambiguity may be too mild a word to describe the strange mixture of great good and frightening evil that our history reveals. And yet, at least until more adequate and probably new words are coined, ambiguity will have to suffice.

Historical ambiguity means that a once seemingly clear historical narrative of progressive Western enlightenment and emancipation has now become a montage of classics and newspeak, of startling beauty and revolting cruelty, of partial emancipation and ever more subtle forms of entrapment. Ambiguous is certainly one way to describe our history and our interpretations of such classics as Exodus. At one time we may have believed realistic and even naturalistic narratives of the triumphs of the West. But these traditional narratives are now overlaid not only with modernist narratives and their occasional epiphanies amidst the mass of historical confusion, but also by post-modernist anti-narratives with their goodbyes to all that.

We find ourselves, therefore, with a *plurality of interpretations of Exodus.* We find ourselves with diverse religious classics among many religious traditions. We find ourselves glimpsing the plurality within each tradition of interpretation while also admitting the ambiguity of every interpretation: liberating possibilities to be retrieved, errors to be criticised, unconscious distortions to be unmasked.

The attempt to understand remains an effort to *interpret well.* But to interpret as pluralistic, ambiguous, and important a phenomenon as the paradigm of Exodus is to enter a *conflict of interpretations* from which there can often seem no exit. The conflicts on how to interpret any religious classic, the conflicts caused by the opposing claims of the religions themselves, and the internal conflicts within any great religion, these all affect interpreters whether they will it or not. None of these conflicts is easily resolved, and no claim to certainty, whether religionist or secularist, should pretend otherwise.

We can continue to give ourselves over to the great hope of Western reason, including the hope for adequate interpretation. But that hope is now a more modest one as a result of the discovery of the *plurality of both language and knowledge and the ambiguities of all histories,* including the history of reason itself. And yet that hope of reason—a hope expressed, for Westerners, in the models of conversation, argument, and interpretation first created by the Greeks—still lives through any honest fidelity to the classic Socratic imperative: 'The unreflective life is not worth living.'

We can continue to give ourselves over to the *great hope alive in the Exodus narrative:* a trust in God as acting for the total liberation of humankind, a hope for our free ability to resist what must be resisted; a hope, if necessary, in hope itself; a hope which, like Exodus, fights against many post-modern exhausted notions of what hope might be. For most religious believers, that Exodus hope arises from the belief that God is grace-ful and will enter into covenant with an empowered, transformed people who will struggle for freedom and liberation. For secular interpreters of Exodus that hope may be glimpsed in the text by sensing some enlightenment, however tentative, and some utopian possibility of emancipation, however modest—as Ernst Bloch taught all to do anew with the text of Exodus and the prophets.

As for the rest, there is no release for any of us from the conflict of interpretations on this central symbol of Exodus if we would understand Judaism or Christianity or Western culture at all. The alternative is not an escape into the transient pleasures of irony, or a flight into despair and cynicism or more history-as-usual. The alternative is not a new kind of innocence or a passivity masking apathy. What Exodus teaches *all* includes this: *Whoever fights for hope, fights on behalf of us all*, whoever acts on that hope in concrete historical and political struggle acts in a manner worthy of a human being. And whoever so acts, acts in a manner faintly suggestive of the reality and power of that God in whose image human beings were formed to resist, to think, and to act: that God-of-Exodus who calls oppressed individuals and peoples even now—to struggle, in the wilderness for years if necessary, in firm hope of the promised land ahead.

3. THE INTERPRETATION OF THE 'PREFERRED ONES'

There are many exemplary scholarly studies of Exodus. But even more than is the case with most religious classics, we also need to hear the interpretations of Exodus by the oppressed and marginalised peoples, the 'preferred ones' of the God of Exodus.

How those preferred ones read the scriptural texts in their own situation becomes imperative for all interpreters to hear. It was, after all, the Black slaves, not their White masters, who rightly interpreted the heart of the liberation narrative of Exodus. God's option for the poor is central to the scriptures. This is not to say that option for the poor is translatable into the distinct claim that only the poor can provide proper readings of these texts, any more than it suggests that only the poor can experience revelation or find salvation, or only the poor are the objects of that radical love of neighbour which is the heart of the Christian Gospel. That option does not translate into the position that says, once the poor make their interpretations, all others are to sit back and passively receive them. In that case, are these new and conflictual readings heard at all? Such passive receptions are engendered by conflict, fear, and guilt, not responsibility. They mask a patronising anxiety which is the forgotten underside of all élite claims to mastery and control.

The option for the poor does translate, however, into the insistence that the *readings of the oppressed must be heard, and preferably heard first*. In terms of the Scripture's own standards, the oppressed are the ones most likely to hear clearly the full religious and political demands of the prophets. Among our contemporaries, their readings are those the rest of us most need to hear. Through their interpretations and actions we can finally read these texts with new eyes and thereby free ourselves from all idealist readings. The mystical-political texts of the prophets and Exodus insist upon *both spiritual and material liberation*. Recall the prophet's judgments on Israel for its treatment of widows, orphans, and the poor; recall the New Testament's portrayal of Jesus as the friend of the outcasts of his day. Christian salvation is not exhausted by any programme of political liberation, to be sure, but Christian salvation, rightly understood, cannot be divorced from the struggle for total human liberation—individual, social, political and religious.

As these new readings by and for the oppressed are heard by all theologians, and, in principle, by all interpreters of religion, a yet deeper sense of our own plurality and ambiguity will surface and give rise to further conflicts of interpretations over the religious classics. Beyond the questions of the sexism, racism, classism, and anti-semitism in the Christian classics and their history of effects upon all interpretations, lies a further disturbing question: Is there yet another illusion systemically operative in much theological discourse—the belief, rarely expressed, but often acted upon, that *only a learned élite can read these texts properly*? For these texts are 'our' property. All who wish to enter the discussion should leave the 'margins' and come to the centres to receive the proper credentials. They must earn properly rights if they are to fashion proper readings of the religious classics.

This kind of unconscious élitism, I have come to believe, is not mere error. Like other distortions, élitism is both unconscious and systemic. It is a distortion whose power will be broken only when we learn to hear these alternative readings of the oppressed. The most powerful acts of resistance are often those where the first lesson is to resist oneself. Many interpreters of religion have begun to learn that lesson on racism, sexism, classism, and anti-semitism. It is time to learn the same kind of lesson on élitism. Exodus can teach us all that anew—especially the interpretations of Exodus by the poor throughout history. The role of the academic theologian, like that of all post-modern intellectuals, needs to learn better ways to hear these new voices. Through attending to the readings and actions by the oppressed of Exodus, we others may learn to become, not alienated egos, but human subjects in active solidarity with all those others we have too often presumed to speak for: that, too, is part of the great narrative of Exodus.

José Severino Croatto

The Socio-historical and Hermeneutical Relevance of the Exodus

THE EXODUS is one of the richest and most fruitful themes in biblical and Judaeo-Christian tradition. Its fruitfulness is seen within the Bible itself: its 'memory' reappears in the Credos of the Israelites, in the legal texts, in the prologues to the Alliances, in hymns and liturgical canticles, in the prophetic texts (of both denunciation and promise) and in the later Wisdom literature (such as the midrash of Wisdom 10–19). It is also recalled in the historical accounts of revelation (such as, for example, Judges 6:8ff; 1 Sam. 10:18; 12:6–8; Josh. 9:9) and in the New Testament use of the vocabulary of 'redemption/liberation/salvation'. This permanence and re-creation of the theme in biblical writings in itself constitutes a noteworthy hermeneutical fact. Furthermore, the biblical *text* of the Exodus has, because of its kerygmatic and theological importance, been a source of inspiration to historical movements that in some way identified themselves with the experience of Israel.

So it seems fitting that this issue should close with a *critical evaluation of the perennial relevance of the Exodus* and of the hermeneutical relevance of movements inspired by it for biblical interpretation. This supposes that the reader will already have studied the preceding analyses of aspects of the Bible and history (past and contemporary). In principle, putting 'Bible' and 'history' together will always be a *historical* statement. The task then is to determine what is permanent and can serve as a model for future liberation processes. Its 'history' (that of the biblical text and of the movements that use the Exodus theme) thus becomes the archetype for new events. The question is: does the Exodus have a permanent relevance, particularly in relation to the future? What gives the kerygma of the Exodus its permanent validity? Is the biblical text something static, a 'type' whose impressions and effects in history are always the same? In other words, what is the *hermeneutical* relevance of the use made of the Exodus in history to interpretation of the biblical text?

It is not the 'outer' aspect of 'Exodus' that confers relevance on the subject and the biblical texts that mention or repeat it. The return from the Babylonian captivity or the return of the Jews to the State of Israel both had the same character of 'Exodus'; most of the processes that have fed on the message of the Exodus, however, have not been 'goings out' from a place of captivity to 'go' to a place of freedom, but acts of *liberation* in the same place in which internal or external domination was being experienced. Some 'goings out' have been purely spiritual—such as the Chiliastic sects. So we are concerned with evaluating the biblical theme of 'exodus' as *liberating event*. Putting the external form of the Israelite Exodus on a secondary level is in itself a significant hermeneutical step. In effect, what lasts in re-readings is not the external factualness of the archetypal event but its underlying *meaning*, its capacity to awaken human reserves of hope in new processes of liberation.

The Exodus event—it does not matter how much of what is related actually 'happened'—released and releases meaning to the extent that it enters into *a process of hermeneutical circularity with socio-historical practice*. This is my basic thesis, which rests on three supports:

(*a*) there is a normative *text*, understood as the kerygma of liberation, which consists not only of the account given in Exodus 1–15 but also of the 'exodus' theme as it appears throughout the Bible;

(*b*) as happened in the case of the history of Israel, so also in the history of the human race over the last two thousand years, there has been and there still is a recourse to this theme *in contexts of liberation*;

(*c*) 'Exodus' and processes of liberation confer meaning on each other. This gives expression to the kernel of the hermeneutical fact, which is empty when there is no build-up of meaning. The subject raises important critical questions.

1. THE PERMANENT RELEVANCE OF THE EXODUS PARADIGM

Why does the Exodus theme run through so many pages of the Bible? What makes it the kerygmatic nucleus of the OT (summed up in 'I am Yahweh, who brought you out of the land of Egypt')? Why is the paschal mystery expressed in the NT with so many images that evoke the Exodus (*áfesis/lútrosis* = remission/ransom)?

The religious and national consciousness of Israel was originally marked out by experiences of oppression and suffering, and of liberation and joy. Reading these experiences from the standpoint of faith led to the *formation of a religious language* that became as central as the historical experiences themselves. Concomitantly, Israel came to affirm a consciousness of freedom as part of its being, and reclaimed its liberation every time it found itself oppressed, as it frequently was in its history. Furthermore, it came to define its God, Yahweh, as 'saviour' and liberator. This is why in Exod. 3:13–14 the text explains the meaning of the name Yahweh as 'I am who am (with you)'. This account is not that of the revelation of the divine name, which was already known, but of the theological connection between this and the Exodus, through the assonance of the name with the formula of protection, 'I shall be with you' of v. 12.[1] This means that the *very name of the God of Israel is indissolubly bound up with the Exodus experience of oppression-liberation*. This can also lead to a new understanding of the expression in Exodus 20:2: 'I am Yahweh your God who brought you out of the land of Egypt, out of the house of slavery'. Besides being a 'memory' of the Exodus, at no less a point than the prologue to the alliance, it is a definition of Yahweh as the one who 'brought out of Egypt'. In other words, the Exodus is not only incorporated in the great texts, which are a reflection of many-layered historical experience, but also in the very name of 'Yahweh'. And therefore any expression of faith and worship is an implicit recalling of the Exodus.[2]

So deep does Old Testament language of liberation run that the NT, despite its spiritualising overtones (the fruit of the transitory context of the early Christian communities), has kept the liberation vocabulary stemming from the Exodus theme. Its application of it to interior, juridical or existential realities (sin, the law, death) is a deepening but not a replacement of the socio-historical reference of the OT. This is confirmed by the fact that the proclamation of the Beatitudes takes up a basic OT theme (Yahweh, defender of the oppressed) and that the initiation of Jesus' ministry in Galilee is presented in Luke 4:16–22 as defined by his option for the poor and the downtrodden.

The creative and varied re-expression of the Exodus theme within the Bible indicates the pre-eminence of the *meaning* of the Exodus over the *event*, and this in turn becomes a norm of interpretation for us. In the life of Israel, no oppression-liberation event could be identical to their experience in Egypt. But the continual recourse to this (to the Exodus) went on building up its symbolic and challenging richness. It was *as though the Exodus embodied all processes of liberation*. So it came to represent the *founding event* of all liberation. As such, it had to go on acquiring ever more relevance and ever greater validity. So there is nothing strange in the fact that later liberation movements have taken their inspiration from the exodus as *paradigm*. There is still—and it needs to be said—a virtually abysmal distance between spiritualistic and pietistic readings of the Exodus, which are regressive and outside the continuum of the experience of Israel, and readings such as those made by theologies of liberation, which add to the kerygmatic nucleus of the Exodus by pointing in the direction of integral liberation (socio-political, religious and spiritual) of the oppressed.

It might be objected that this elevation of the Exodus to the rank of paradigm of liberation, and the selective utilisation of the OT that goes with it, amounts to choosing 'a canon within the canon'. Well, all reading of the Bible is selective. A text with so many different theological strands, containing so many different literary genres, cannot but be too extensive and changing to be read all in the same way. Also, tradition has always read the Bible by placing greater emphasis on certain passages. What we should be suspicious of is the way the socio-historical projection of its kerygma, as applied to the Exodus, has been ignored at critical moments or in certain theological currents. What is plain, in any case, is that any Christian recourse to the Exodus has to be from a 'christological' viewpoint, which does not mean blocking out the OT. Its kerygma retains its full validity but is complemented by the viewpoint of the NT.

But if the Bible itself includes so many other accounts of liberation events, why give the Exodus such pre-eminence? There are several ways of answering this:

(a) It was (or is presented by the texts as) *an original event*, and one that was decisive for the creation of Israel as a free people; what is original acquires *a foundational character* and takes on a unique prestige. This is why the Exodus is sometimes told in 'creational' language (Isa. 51:9–10; Ps. 74:12–15) and the Targumic tradition connects Exodus-creation with the two first sacred nights of creation.

(b) The first liberation is *linked to the first Passover*; when this feast acquired special relevance, in deuteronomic theology, the Exodus was also more deeply entrenched in Israelite consciousness. The Passover, in effect, was the 'memorial' (*zikkaron*) of the going out from Egypt. In this way, worship and socio-historical practice were united and mutually reinforced.

(c) What fascinates the narrator of the Exodus is Yahweh's *option for the oppressed*. The oppression and exploitation of the people are described in great detail (Exod. 1–6), enhancing the contrast between these and the account of their setting free: this account is not generic but refers to a specific situation, which can easily be picked up in others. Compare it, for example, with the account of the exile. There is no text there describing the social and economic situation of the Israelites or Jews in the conquering nations of Assyria and Babylon. The accounts stress the destruction of Samaria and Jerusalem and

their respective kingdoms, and therefore also (in the case of Judah) the return
to the city and the rebuilding of its fabric and institutions. But the exile itself is
not described as Israel's captivity in Egypt is.

(*d*) For this reason, and because it is not an original event, it is rather the
exile that has light shed on it by the Exodus, as this has by cosmogony, as in
Isa. 51:9–11 and, without mentioning the creation, 11:10–16 and Ps. 74:12–15.

(*e*) The Exodus event has an obvious *political and social content*. Its
political aspect (the domination of the Hebrews by an alien power which keeps
them in captivity in order to serve it) takes on transcendent overtones, through
the solemn confrontation between two divine powers, that of the Egyptian
gods (represented by Pharaoh), and that of Yahweh. The social aspect is
contained in the condition of slaves experienced by the Israelites in the land of
Egypt. The two aspects are bound up together, as the stereotyped phrase of the
legal and alliance texts proclaims: 'I am Yahweh, your God, who brought you
out of the land of *Egypt*, out of the house of *bondage*'. Whether it is servitude
in a foreign and imperialist land, or servitude imposed in their own land by a
foreign, imperialist power (as under the Persians, see Nehemiah 9:36–7), the
political and social content˜is the same. The Israelites experienced many
situations of foreign oppression, as the historical books relate, with social and
economic results that are not hard to deduce. But they also experienced social
oppression from their own ruling powers. This is constantly measured by
reference to the overwhelming experience in Egypt. The challenge,
'Remember that you were a slave (or foreigner) in the land of Egypt', is
deliberately repeated in legal prescriptions with a social content (Deut. 15:15;
24:18–22; Exod. 22:20; 23:9; Lev. 19:34, 36), and is paraphrased by the
prophets most critical of social injustice (Amos 3:1ff.; Mic. 6:4; Jer. 2:1ff.).
This is why the picture of the oppression of the Hebrews in Egypt and the
account of their liberation from it has had such a powerful and fruitful impact
on the life of Israel and of oppressed groups in all ages. The Exodus, therefore,
became the *founding event* not only for the course of Israelite history, but also,
through its kerygmatic appropriation, for *other oppressed communities*. In
other words, its foundational character is continually being reinforced
through so many re-readings, a sure sign of its richness as a source.

(*f*) A further indication of the paradigmatic character of the Exodus is the
surprising verbal formulations it receives in *liturgical and hymnic recall:*
Yahweh is defined as '(he who) brings (*not* 'brought' as in so many
translations) Israel out of Egypt': see Ps. 136:11 (the creation and beginning of
salvation history are recounted with nine participles in vv. 4–16); Isa. 43:16ff.;
63:11 ('where is he who brings (them) out of the sea?'). This is done because the
Exodus is an archetypal event, because its efficacy is felt to belong to the
present; so Yahweh is defined as the God of '*permanent* exodus/liberation'.

All these convergent aspects of the kerygmatic continuance of the Exodus during three thousand years of experiences of oppression and processes of liberation have a significant theological force. They show just what the identity of the biblical God is and that of his saving plan which is *first expressed* on the socio-historical level. Taking up the experience of the God of the Exodus today means *fighting in his name against all forms of injustice and oppression*. So the historical relevance of the Exodus is far from over. On the contrary, its paradigmatic and foundational character is increased in the measure that it is reappropriated as a religious symbol in present-day liberation struggles. Our improved present understanding of the mechanisms of domination, dependency and oppression brings with it a greater intensity of light shed by the Exodus.

Finally, it must be said that the hermeneutical appropriation of the Exodus by theologies of liberation concerned with socio-political or cultural questions has put a stop to the other, individualistic and spiritualistic, appropriations of it made by earlier centuries. Today, it is those that appear to reduce the significance of the Exodus.

2. THE HERMENEUTICAL RELEVANCE OF CONTEMPORARY LIBERATION MOVEMENTS FOR THE INTERPRETATION OF THE BIBLE

In my opening paragraph I looked at the energising and illuminating continuance of the Exodus theme in the movements it inspired and in processes and theologies of liberation. Let us now look at the inverse effect: whether those movements and processes have influenced interpretation of the Bible. This is posing the hermeneutical problem, advancing our thesis that, in order to complete the hermeneutical circle, the biblical kerygma of exodus/liberation should *grow* in meaning, and that this growth should also affect other texts and our understanding of the whole Bible. Let us briefly examine the questions raised.

(a) The Bible is not a 'deposit' of revelation, from which ever identical contents can be drawn out. This is an archaic, anti-hermeneutical concept, which can only be sustained by an academic, doctrinaire or authoritarian reading of the Bible. The 'learned', the academics, those who hold power in the Church, are not those who decide the meaning of the biblical text. Their contribution is minimal, however great it may be on the technical level. *The authentic reading of the biblical message is done from socio-historical practice*, from where faith discovers God acting. In the case of the Exodus as paradigm for movements of liberation, this means that they are what help towards a deeper understanding of its salvific meaning, and they are what make this *grow*.

Any reading in fact, far from being an *ex*traction of the fixed meaning of a text (the traditional concept of *ex*egesis), is a *production of meaning*. Linguistics and semiotics, as well as hermeneutics, contribute to this, as I have analysed elsewhere.[3] Therefore, any reading of the biblical theme of the Exodus done from within situations of oppression and processes or movements of liberation, is an exploration of its reserves of meaning, of its inexhaustible fruitfulness. It is a *re*-reading, which implies reinterpreting the archetypal event so that it tunes in with new events. It is an *eis*egetical act. Contrary to what is often heard in academic circles (where there is much knowledge of the *history* of the texts), *eisegesis is the obverse of exegesis, not a distortion of it*. Any reading, even that which claims to be neutral or 'scientific', is eisegetical before being exegetical. And the texts that develop the theme of liberation, so well summed up in the account of the Exodus, have no better readers than the oppressed who seek their own liberation. Academics can tell us everything about the past of a text (its context, authorship, the traditions on which it draws, etc.), but the oppressed can, from their practice of liberation, give us the 'unspoken' aspect of what the text says; that is, its present kerygmatic value.

(*b*) I have said that any reading of a text is a production (not a reproduction or repetition) of its meaning. It is a *re*-reading. This implies a re-contextualisation too. Modern methods of historical criticism are an enormous help in contextualising the production of a text, and often of its underlying strata. This is splendid work, both worthwhile and necessary. But it *only* converts reading of a biblical text into 'history' of the text: what it meant at such a time and in such a cultural context. There is a risk of fossilising this 'situated' meaning. Linguistic sciences, however, show that both the author and the recipient of a text, as well as their surroundings, change rapidly. We find this easy to allow with regard to the original recipient and context, less easy with regard to the author. But the author *dies* in the very act of producing his work. When we read, we read a text and not (or only indirectly) an author.

The loss of author, recipient and 'world' of a text (though we may know them through analysing their work) leaves us alone *with the text*, whose message has to be deciphered through the same rules of language as served for its codification. But it is also the case that any text is *monosemic* in its production (its author wants to say something to someone about something), but not once it becomes distanced from the moment of its production. It becomes *polysemic* through the disappearance of those three elements that defined its meaning and through the complexity of its codes, which allow new access to it from many standpoints. So its reading from another cultural standpoint, by other recipients, without the regulating presence of the author, is a *re*-reading, a new definition of its meaning that has no reason to coincide with the original reading. *To interpret is to create, not to repeat.* A conductor interpreting a symphony is not repeating its first broadcast but drawing new possibilities of meaning out of the text handed down to him. One is being more faithful to a text by recreating it than by claiming to re-transmit its original message, which is in any case impossible to do.

Linguistics distinguishes between the meaning of a text (what it says semantically) and its referent (what it refers to outside itself). The Bible is a message for what it *says* as a text, not for what it 'said' at the time it was written. So, for example, we can debate, as critics, about the referent of Isa. 53 (Joaquim, Zorobabel, Israel, a prophet?) but the message of this text does not depend solely on being able to establish this. It has just as much meaning when seen as polysemic—more so, in fact, without the original referent. The New Testament re-contextualised it, giving it a christological referent, thereby elevating this passage to the status of hermeneutical key to the paschal mystery. So oppressed peoples can also re-appropriate its 'meaning' by putting themselves as new referents. In this way the meaning *grows*; so re-reading becomes a creative act; so Isa. 53 has a new relevance when it is read from the world of the oppressed.

The same happens to the Exodus theme. The specialist is concerned with reconstructing 'what happened' at the time, or discovering how tradition was transformed (part of the hermeneutical process!) till it took shape in the text as we have it. Perhaps he can also add the 'the history of the exegesis' of the text of the Book of Exodus. But doing this does not make its meaning grow, however useful the task might be. The meaning of the original Exodus went on growing through the re-readings or appropriations of meaning that Israel made of it in its experiences of oppression and liberation; through the reinterpretations coming from historical movements that appealed to it without reducing it to a purely spiritual event; and it grows now through being taken up by contemporary theologies of liberation springing not from books but from the *practice* of liberation. These new re-readings expand and actualise the meaning of the Exodus, and make it still more paradigmatic for future generations, who in their turn will make use of it in ways we cannot know.

The movements and processes that appeal to the Exodus of the Bible as the motive force behind their practice of liberation make us realise that the Bible is a message to the extent that it is re-contextualised and re-read; that it is not a static and universal 'word of God', an archaic deposit of revelation, but a norm for the understanding of *where God is revealing himself* today. This in itself would be enough to correct certain theological distortions (concepts of revelation and the 'word of God') and exegetical ones (fixation on the 'historical' meaning of the texts). Critical exegesis—which has left fundamentalist and authoritarian readings of the Bible without a leg to stand on—is valuable for the amazing light it has been able to shed on the texts. But to stay at this point is bringing the past back to life; what is needed is rather to clear the way for a hermeneutical enrichment, for a reading of the texts on the basis of present reality. And if this reading is to correspond to reality, it has to be made from within human processes. Just so, the theme of the Exodus is *recreated* from within the processes and struggles for liberation by oppressed or dominated peoples and communities.

And if the paradigmatic value of the Exodus has been so influential in the life of Israel and in contemporary movements and processes of liberation, its retroactive influence on interpretation of the Bible can be no less. This is what gives it its hermeneutical relevance.

Translated by Paul Burns

Notes

1. See J. S. Croatto 'Yo soy el que estoy (contigo). La interpretación del nombre de "Yahvé" en Ex. 3:13–14' in V. Collado and E. Zurro *El misterio de la palabra* (Madrid 1983) pp. 147–159.

2. For this reason it is regrettable that Jewish tradition has marginalised this name rendering it unpronounceable, and that, via the Septuagint, this confessional regression should have passed to the NT and the bulk of Christian tradition.

3. *Biblical Hermeneutics: towards a Theory of Reading as Production of Meaning* (Maryknoll 1986).

Contributors

GREGORY BAUM was born in Berlin in 1923 and has lived in Canada since 1940. He pursued his studies at McMaster University, Hamilton, Canada, Ohio State University, USA, Fribourg University, Switzerland and the New School for Social Research in New York, USA. He is Master of Arts and Doctor of Theology, and is currently professor of theology at St Michael's College in Toronto University. He is editor of *The Ecumenist* and his publications include *Man Becoming* (1970), *New Horizon* (1972), *Religion and Alienation* (1975), *The Social Imperative* (1978), *Catholics and Canadian Socialism* (1980), *The Priority of Labor* (1982) and *Ethics and Economics* (1984).

DIANNE BERGANT, CSA is Associate Professor of Old Testament Studies at Catholic Theological Union in Chicago. She is the editor of The Bible Today and general editor of the *Collegeville Bible Commentary* (OT series), all of which are published by the Liturgical Press. Her publications include: *Job & Ecclesiastes* (1982); *What Are They Saying About Wisdom Literature?* (1984); *An Introduction to the Bible* (1985). She served on the Commission on Faith and Order for the National Council of Churches (1979–85) and the committee that produced *An Inclusive Language Lectionary* under the auspices of that same National Council.

RITA BURNS works in the Department of Religious Studies, Saint Mary's College, Notre Dame, Indiana. She gained a master's degree in Hebrew and Semitic Studies from the University of Wisconsin at Madison, Wisconsin, and a doctorate in Religious Studies (Scripture) from Marquette University in Milwaukee, Wisconsin. Her publications include: *Exodus, Leviticus, Numbers with Excursus on Feasts, Ritual and Typology*. Old Testament Message (1983); *Ezra and Nehemiah*. Collegeville Bible Commentary (1985).

JAY S. CASEY is a graduate of the Southern Baptist Theological Seminary, Louisville, Kentucky, and is currently pastor of the Lake Norman Baptist Church, Huntersville, North Carolina.

JOSÉ SEVERINO CROATTO was born in 1930. A Catholic, he teaches Old Testament studies at the Evangelical Institute of Higher Theological Studies in Buenos Aires. He holds degrees from the Pontifical Biblical Institute in Rome and the Hebrew University of Jerusalem. His 'History of Salvation', first published in 1966, is in its seventh edition and has been translated into Italian and Dutch. Among his books translated into English are *Exodus: a Hermeneutics of Freedom* (1981) and *Biblical Hermeneutics: towards a Theory of Reading as Production of Meaning* (1986).

ENRIQUE DUSSEL holds doctorates in philosophy (Madrid) and history (Sorbonne) and a licenciate in theology (Paris), and in 1981 was awarded an honorary doctorate in theology by the University of Fribourg. He is professor of the history of Latin American theology and the Latin American church at ITES in Mexico and a professor of the National Autonomous University of Mexico (UNAM). He is also president of the commission for the study of the history of the Church in Latin America (CEHILA), and coordinator of the corresponding commission in the Ecumenical Association of Third World Theologians (EATWOT), and a member of the executive of the International Association of Mission Studies (IAMS). Among Professor Dussel's recent works are *History of the Church in Latin America. Colonialism to Liberation (1492–1979)* (1981); *Philosophy of Liberation* (1985); *Introducción general a la Historia de la Iglesia en América Latina*, I/1 (1983); *La producción teórica de Marx. Una introducción a los Grundrisse*, Siglo XXI (1985); *Caminhos de libertação latino-americana*, I: *Interpretação histórico-teológica*, II: *Historia, Colonialismo e Libertação*, III: *Interpretação ético-teológica*, IV: *Reflexões para una Teologia da Libertação* (1985); *Ética communitaria*, collection 'Teologia y Liberación' VIII (1986).

WESLEY A. KORT is professor of religion at Duke University in Durham, North Carolina, USA. He received his undergraduate degrees from Calvin College and Calvin Theological Seminary and his graduate degrees from the University of Chicago. Before coming to Duke University, he taught in the Department of Religion at Princeton University. In addition to many articles concerning the relation of literature and literary theory to religion and theology, he has written four books: *Shriven Selves: Religious Problems in Recent American Fiction* (1972), *Narrative Elements and Religious Meaning* (1975), *Moral Fiber: Character and Belief in Recent American Fiction* (1982), and *Modern Fiction and Human Time: A Study in Narrative and Belief* (1985).

PINCHAS LAPIDE was born in 1922 in Vienna and migrated to Palestine in 1940. He served in the British Army's Jewish Brigade during the second world war. As a diplomat he spent many years in the service of the Israeli Foreign Ministry. From 1965 to 1971 he was director of the government press office in

Jerusalem. From 1972 to 1975 he was running an institute and was senior lecturer at Bar Ilan University and was also associate professor at the American College in Jerusalem. The years 1975 to 1977 he spent in theological research, from 1977 to 1978 he was visiting lecturer at the Kirchliche Hochschule, Wuppertal, and from 1978 to 1979 visiting professor of New Testament studies at Göttingen. Among his works are: *Brother or Lord?* (with Hans Küng); *Auferstehung: ein jüdisches Glaubenserlebnis; Juden und Christen* (with a foreword by Hans Küng); *Der Jude Jesus* (with Ulrich Luz); *Was Juden und Christen voneinander denken* (with Franz Mussner and Ulrich Wilkens); *Jüdischer Mono-Theismus—christliche Trinitätslehre* (with Jürgen Moltmann).

ROLAND E. MURPHY, OCarm, is the George Washington Ivey Professor of Biblical Studies at Duke University (Durham, NC). He is the co-editor and contributor for *The Jerome Biblical Commentary* studies on biblical subjects.

JOHN A. NEWTON, MA (Cantab.), PhD (Lond), D Litt (Hull), Superintendent Minister of the West London Mission of the Methodist Church of Great Britain, was tutor in Church History, Wesley College, Bristol, between 1967–72, taught Church History at St Paul's United Theological College, Limuru, Kenya, and the University of Nairobi, between 1972–73, was Principal of Wesley College, Bristol, 1973–78, and Recognised Teacher in the University of Bristol. His publications include *Methodism and the Puritans* (1964); *Susanna Wesley and the Puritan Tradition in Methodism* (1968); *The Palestine Problem* (1972); *Search for a Saint: Edward King* (1977).

DAVID TRACY was born in 1939 in Yonkers, New York. He is a priest of the diocese of Bridgeport, Connecticut, and a doctor of theology of the Gregorian University, Rome. He is professor of philosophical theology at the Divinity School of Chicago University. He is the author of *The Achievement of Bernard Lonergan* (1970), *Blessed Rage for Order: New Pluralism in Theology* (1975) and *The Analogical Imagination* (1980). He contributes to several reviews and is editor of the *Journal of Religion* and of the *Religious Studies Review*.

ANTON WEILER was born in 1927 in Voorburg in the Netherlands and studied philosophy and history at Nijmegen University. He has been professor of Universal and Dutch Medieval History and of the Philosophy of History at Nijmegen since 1964 and 1965 respectively. Since 1984, he has been the President and Curator of the Catholic Theological University of Utrecht. In addition to many articles, he has published the following books: *Heinrich von*

Gorkum (1431). Seine Stellung in der Philosophie und der Theologie des Spätmittelalters (1962); *Geschiedenis van de kerk in Nederland* (1963), written together with O. J. de Jong, L. J. Rogier and C. W. Mönnich; *Deus in Terris. Middeleeuwse wortels van de totalitaire ideologie* (1965); *Christelijk bestaan in een seculaire cultuur* (1969), written together with others; *Necrologie, Kroniek en cartularium o. a. van het fraterhuis te Doesburg (1432–1559)* (1974); *Monasticon Windeshemense* Part 3: *Niederlande* (1980), written together with Noël Geirnaert.

JOSIAH U. YOUNG III was born in 1953 in Dayton, Ohio. He obtained his college degree from Morehouse College and finished his education at Union Theological Seminary, where he obtained his doctorate of philosophy. He is Assistant Professor of Philosophy and Religion at Colgate University, Hamilton, NY. Professor Young is the author of *Black and African Theologies: Siblings or Distant Cousins? Toward Pan-African Theology* (1986).

ERICH ZENGER was born in Dollnstein, Bavaria in 1939, and did philosophical, theological and oriental studies in Rome, Jerusalem, Heidelberg and Münster. He is currently Professor of Old Testament Exegesis in the Faculty of Catholic Theology of the University of Münster. His publications include: *Die Sinaitheophanie* (1971); *Exodus. Geschichten und Geschichte der Befreiung Israels* (1982; together with P. Weimar); *Das Buch Exodus* (1982); *Israel am Sinai. Analysen und Interpretationen zu Exodus 17–34* (1985).

CONCILIUM

CONCILIUM

CONCILIUM 1986

All back issues are still in print: available from bookshops (price £4.95) or direct from the publisher (£5.45/US$8.95/Can$10.95 including postage and packing).

T & T CLARK LTD, 59 GEORGE STREET EDINBURGH EH2 2LQ, SCOTLAND